Also by Robin Goldstein

Fearless Critic Houston Restaurant Guide

Fearless Critic Austin Restaurant Guide

The Menu: Restaurant Guide to New Haven

The Menu: Restaurant Guide to Northampton,
Amherst, and the Five-College Area

THE WINE
TRIALS

Fearless Critic Media
Austin, Texas www.fearlesscritic.com

First edition

Printed in the United States of America

ISBN 978-0-9740143-5-7

Authors

Author **Robin Goldstein** is the founder and editor-in-chief of the *Fearless Critic* series. He has authored four books of restaurant reviews and has written for more than 30 *Fodor's* travel guides, from Italy to Thailand, Argentina to Hong Kong. Robin is a graduate of Harvard University and the Yale Law School. He has a certificate in cooking from the French Culinary Institute in New York and a WSET advanced wine and spirits certificate.

Managing Editor **Alexis Herschkowitsch** is a co-author of two *Fearless Critic* restaurant guides. She has also written for the *Fodor's* travel guides to Mexico, Central America, and Thailand. She is a graduate of the University of Texas at Austin, and has a WSET advanced wine and spirits certificate. Alexis co-authored the wine reviews in this book.

Contributing writers

Johan Almenberg, co-author of Appendix 2, is an economist at the Stockholm School of Economics. His research focuses on how social norms and psychological biases affect economic outcomes. **Anna Dreber Almenberg**, co-author of Appendix 2, is an economist at the Stockholm School of Economics and the Program for Evolutionary Dynamics at Harvard University. Her work investigates cooperation and the effects of hormones on economic decisions. **Nat Davis**, author of the "The trials of pouring," is the sommelier of Uchi restaurant in Austin, Texas. **Brian DiMarco**, author of "Five wine myths on trial," is the owner and president of Barter House Imports, a rare and fine wines importer based in New York City. **Jay Emerson**, co-author of Appendix 1, is Assistant Professor of Statistics at Yale University. **Julian Faulkner**, author of "The trials of a young winemaker," runs Le Grand Cros winery and Jules Wines in the south of France. **Jake Katz**, co-author of Appendix 1, is a statistician who has worked with Lehman Brothers and Strategic Value Partners. **Justin Nowell**, director and producer of the Wine Trials video at www.thewinetrials.com, is a New York-based filmmaker whose work has been selected for the Sundance Film Festival.

Scientific advisory board

The following professors and scientists gave generously of their time and professional expertise to support our project, interpret our results, and review our methods and conclusions for scientific accuracy. The opinions set forth in this book do not necessarily reflect the views of any of these advisers or their academic institutions. Fearless Critic Media assumes sole responsibility for all published content; any errors, factual or otherwise, are ours alone.

Editors and contributors

The following people contributed generously to our project in numerous ways: organizing or hosting blind tastings, reviewing our methodology and conclusions, editing and proofreading drafts of the manuscript, and even hosting the authors in their homes. The opinions set forth in this book do not necessarily reflect the views of any of these contributors. Fearless Critic Media assumes sole responsibility for all published content; any errors, factual or otherwise, are ours alone.

Andrea Armeni, Associate Editor
Margarita Barcenas, Event Coordinator
Leah Barton, Event Coordinator
Hal Bayless, Event Coordinator
Nikia Bergan, General Contributor
Adam Brackman, Photographer
Bill Collins, Event Host
Morgan Friedman, General Contributor
Daniel Frommer, Associate Editor
James Frutkin, Associate Editor
Andrew Gajkowski, General Contributor
Navid Ghedami, Event Host
Barry Goldstein, Associate Editor and Event Host
Rosie Goldstein, Event Host
Kacie Gonzalez, Publishing Assistant
David Grossman, Chef
Claudio Guerra, Event Host
Daniel Horwitz, Associate Editor
Bobby Huegel, Mixologist
Roy Ip, Chef and Event Host
Winnie Ip, Event Host
Jeff Kaplan, Event Coordinator
Anat Kaufman, Photographer
David Kim, Event Coordinator
Sidney Kwiram, Associate Editor
Duncan Levin, Associate Editor
Benjamin Lima, Associate Editor
Josh Loving, Event Host

Editors and contributors *continued*

Rebecca Markovits, Associate Editor
Charles Mayes, Event Host
Colin McCarthy, Event Coordinator
Caroline McLean, Event Host
Erin McReynolds, Associate Editor
David Menschel, Associate Editor
Clare Murumba, Event Host
Angie Niles, Event Coordinator
Brane Poledica, Event Host
Isaure de Pontbriand, Associate Editor
Karisa Prestera, Event Host
Benjamin Rosenblum, General Contributor
Daniel Rosenblum, Photographer
Abigail Roth, Event Coordinator
James Saccento, General Contributor
Marcus Samuelsson, Chef and Event Host
Claude Solliard, Chef and Event Host
Kelly Stecker, Publishing Assistant and Photographer
Brian Stubbs, Event Host
Harold Stubbs, Associate Editor
Lu Stubbs, Associate Editor
Susan Stubbs, Associate Editor and Event Host
Cody Taylor, Event Coordinator
Mark Trachtenberg, Event Host
Darya Trapeznikova, Event Coordinator
Andy Vickery, Event Host
Carol Vickery, Event Host
Kent Wang, Web Developer
Justin Yu, General Contributor

Blind tasters

The following people participated in our blind tastings. Tasters not listed here wished to remain anonymous. However, the opinions set forth in this book do not necessarily reflect the views of any of the individual tasters listed below. Fearless Critic Media assumes sole responsibility for all published content.

Suzanne Adelman
Caroline Adler
Bob Agoglia
Ali Ahsan
Frances Aldous-Worley
Elnaz Alipour-Assiabi
Johan Almenberg
Anna Dreber Almenberg
Michael Amendola
Janelle Anderson
Whitney Angstadt
Lorenzo Aragona
Fernando Aramburo
Larinia Arena
Brenda Audino
Laura Austin
Marty Austin
Leila Ayachi
Leigh M. Bailey
Donna L. Balin
Scott A. Balin
David Ball
Nicole Ball
Oleg Balter
Shai Bandner
Margarita Barcenas
Rhondale-Marie Barras
Catherine Barry
Leah Barton
Ben Batchelder
Anne C. Bauer

Nathaniel Baum-Snow
Hal Bayless
Andrew Benner
Zachary Bennett
Steven Bercu
Amber Berend
Edward H. Berman
Julia Berman
Jason Berns
Jennifer Berns
Susan Biancani
Chris Black
J.D. Bloodworth
Rayna Bourke
Vanessa Treviño Boyd
Wood Boyles
Adam Brackman
Uda M. Bradford
Delana Brandon
Benjamin J. Brandow
Kevin Brass
Lietza Brass
Judith Brock
Patrick Brock
Stacey Brock
Aileen B. Brophy
Ezra T. Brown
Jaclynn T. Brown
Joy Brunner
L.R. Brunner
S.S. Brunner

Blind tasters *continued*

Robert Buchele
Thomas Burke
Gary L. Bush
Nancy H. Bush
Matthew J. Caballero
Mark Cabell
Rick Cagney
Michele Camp
Jeff Caplan
Lisa Carley
Ale Carlos
Robert Carroll
Kimberly Casey
Marlon Castillo
Claire Champagne
John Champagne
Zoe Chance
Benjamin Chang
Helen Chong
Gaetan Ciampini
Dennis Clark
John B. Clutterbuck
Suzanna Cole
William M. Collins
Marcus Allen Cooper
Russell W. Cooper
David Cordúa
Denis Costaz
Nadia Croes
Katy Cuddihee
Marc Cuenod
Martha Cuenod
Nat Davis
C.J. Dean
Frank Debons
Jana Demetral
Nisha Desai
Brian J. DiMarco

Shoshana Dobrow
Chezmin N. Dolinsky
Susan K. Dudek
Shaun Duffy
Carol Duke
Seth Dunn
Kenneth Dyer
Julie Sinclair Eakin
James Endicott
Joel Ephross
Matt Epstein
Sarah Escobar
Samantha Essen
Julie Fairbanks
Virginia H. Fallon
Julian Faulkner
Amy E. Ferrer
Monica Fields
Ben Fieman
Cristina Finan
Paul Flores
Sharla Flores
Christine Folch
Eric Foret
Ana Fox
Judd Frankel
Shane Frederick
John Freeman
Sylvia Freeman
Morgan Friedman
Marika Frumes
Jim Frutkin
Eleni Gage
Andrew Gajkowski
Jessica L. Gant
Seanna Garrison
Thomas J. Garza
Marva Gay

Robert Gerstle
Jeffrey Giles
Julie Goldman
Barry Goldstein
Maria J. Gomez
Nick Gossett
Michelle Grasso
Ed Greenbaum
Claire Liu Greenberg
Seth Grossman
Frederic Guarino
Elaine Gubbins
Megan G. Gubbins
Claudio Guerra
Elisabeth Gutowski
John Ha
Casey Dué Hackney
Ryan Hackney
Lauren Hale
Deb Hall
William Erin Hall
Mike Handel
Tracie Handel
Michelle S. Hardy
Joan Harmon
Amy K. Harper
Elizabeth W. Harries
Brian Hay
Monica Hayes
Kristen Hendricks
Jodie Hermann
David Hesse
Leslie Hill
Ed Hirs
Steven Hite
Stacey Holman
Ellen Horne
Pamela Horton
Daniel Horwitz
Jenny Howe

Lee-Sean Huang
Tasneem Husain
Alexandra Hynes
Roy Ip
Reena Isaac
Karen G. Jackson
Tim Jensen
Beverly Jernigan
Josean Jimenez
Alexis Johnson
Ali Jouzdani
Eirini Kaissaratou
Jeff Kaplan
Laurence A. Kaplan
Jake Katz
Michael G. Katz
Anat Kaufman
Alexandra Kaufmann
Sarah Kelly
Emily Kelsch
Samantha Kennedy
Nina Kiernan
David Kim
Allison Kirby
Lauren Klein
Sarah K. Kozlowski
Alison Kriviskey
Bruce M. Kriviskey
Tim Kutach
Dea Larson
Nichole Byrne Lau
Samantha Lazarus
Eugene Lee
Risha Lee
Jennifer A. Lee
Kari Leeper
Amelia Lester
Michael Levi
Duncan Levin
Steve Levine

Blind tasters *continued*

Benjamin Lima
Kristin Lindner
Jes Logan
Matthew Lombardi
Stephen G. Long
Ayanna Lonian
Natalie Louie
Josh Loving
Ginger Lowry
Jennifer Luddy
Kerry Lusignan
Jane Baxter Lynn
Zachary Mallavia
Will Manlove
Edward T. Mannix, III
Paul A. Mardas
Olga Gonzalez Marruffo
Andrea Marsh
Jonathan Martel
Moira Bessette Martin
Thomas Martin
Dan Martinez
Beth Martinez
Tom McCasland
Lindsey McCormack
Sally McDaniel
Caroline McLean
Megan McMahon
Walter J. McMahon
Erin McReynolds
Michael Macedo Meazell
Elsa Mehary
Ferne Mele
David Menschel
Elizabeth Merrill
Christiane Metral
Charles H. Michelet
George I. Miller

Jaclyn Miller
Samantha Miller
Julie Mischlich
Tejal Mody
Dorothy Molnar
Amy E. Moran
Chris Mrema
Matthias Mueller
Clare Kogire Murumba
Luke Murumba
Keren Murumba
Matthew Murumba
Samuel Murumba
Vinay B. Nair
Joe Napolitano
Stew Navarre
Daniel Nelson
Monika Powe Nelson
Catherine New
Martin A. Nowak
Justin Nowell
Thomas Nowell
Louis Orenstein
Anne Ouimette
Debbie Padon
Tom Pappalardo
William Parra
Lisa Parrish
Akshay Patil
Drew Patterson
Elizabeth Morrison Petegorsky
Stephen Petegorsky
Isaure de Pontbriand
Charles B. Powers
Ron Prashker
Jennie Pries
Risher Randall
Andrea Ranft

Greg Ranft
Ofir Reichenberg
Taj Reid
Julee Resendez
George Reynolds
Elizabeth Richmond-Garza
Matt Rigney
Bob A. Rivollier
Gerrit Rogers
Medora M. Rogers
Patrick Rohan
Kayla Rosenberg
Benjamin Rosenblum
Daniel Rosenblum
Murry Rosenblum
Debbie Rosmarin
Jori Ross
Elizabeth A. Rovere
Mary Pat Roy
Michael J. Roy
Denise Ruhl
James Saccento
Kate Drake Saccento
Jane Sackett
M. Melinda Sanders
Sherri Sandifer
Susan Sandikcioglu
Jorge Sanhueza-Lyon
Ruben Sanz Ramiro
Sue Schmidt
Tatiana Schnur
Peter Schultz
Joseph A. Sena, Jr.
Taylor Senatore
Rachel Shiffrin
Erin Sibley
Jeff Siegel
Leslie Silbert
Will Silverman
Mark Simmelkjaes

Emily Singer
Alison D. Smith
Sarah Smith
Michael Sobolevsky
John P. Sobolweski
Claude A. Solliard
Linda K. Sparks
Joel Spiro
Ashley St. Clair
Chanel Eve Stark
Kelly Stecker
Judith Stinson
Robert C. Stinson
Brian Stubbs
Sue Stubbs
Kari Sullivan
Marty Sullivan
Linda Summers
Sara Jane Summers
Adam Taplin
Laura Tatum
Cody Taylor
Mary Taylor
Andrew Teich
Antonia Thomas
Elana Thurston-Milgrom
Melissa Tischler
Eric Titner
Anne Todd
Bruce Tolda
Darya Trapeznikova
Cynthia Urrutia
Justin Vann
Holly M. Veech
Alan Verson
Matt Verson
Paula Verson
A. Vora
Preeya Vyas
Johannes Walker

Blind tasters *continued*

Brad Wall
Ruth Waser
Jillian Wein
Thomas Weiner
Andrew Whitcomb
Kirk Wickline
Cynthia M. Williams
Lisa Michelle Wilmore
Elsie E. Wilmoth
Rae Wilson
Clarence Wine
Matt Wong
Betty Yip
Randy Yost
Richard Young
Justin Yu
George R. Zimmerman
Donald H. Zuckerman
Donna E. Zuckerman
Monwabisi Zukani

Contents

People

Authors and contributing writers v
Scientific advisory board vi
Editors and contributors vii
Blind tasters ix

The Wine Trials

Preface: The wine haze 1
Chapter 1: Blind taste 7
Chapter 2: The taste of money 11
Chapter 3: The perfect palate? 15
Chapter 4: Dom Pérignon's new clothes 19
Chapter 5: So what? 25
Chapter 6: The culture war 31
Chapter 7: Our wine trials 39
Chapter 8: Your wine trials 49
Chapter 9: The verdict 55
Notes 59

100 recommended wines under $15

Winning wines and editors' picks 63
List of recommended wines by style 64
Wine reviews 67

Appendices

Appendix 1: Experimental design .175
Appendix 2: Experimental conclusions 179

Index 183

The Wine Trials

Preface The wine haze

College students are often paired with cheap wine, so it's fitting that the idea for this book can be traced back to my senior year at college, when three classmates and I were living in a six-room suite in Harvard's Dunster House. Four bedrooms plus a common room left us with one extra room, and as any four rational, single 21-year-old men would have done, we decided to turn it into a bar.

My suite-mates Dan, Nick, Ben, and I bought wood, dark stain, hinges, and the glossiest varnish we could find at Home Depot. We made use of the circular saw in an underpublicized woodshop hidden in the Dunster House basement. We built and installed liquor shelves backed by mirrors. We put up Christmas lights and candles, and we printed a bar menu. Our only real wall adornments were a mask and a spear that Dan had brought back from his homeland of South Africa, so we named it the Mask and Spear Pub.

Charging for drinks at the bar would have been illegal and, worse, impractical. Instead, when we opened for business, we accepted bottle donations from our patrons. Each endowed bottle would be embossed with the name of its patron (e.g. "The David F. Elmer Bottle of Sweet Vermouth," donated by one of our regulars), and customers would be required to toast that patron when drinking from his or her endowed bottle.

By the second month of the Mask and Spear's short lifetime, we had hundreds of customers and dozens of endowed bottles. The Dunster House disciplinarian, known as a "senior tutor," wasn't thrilled with the situation. He attempted various methods to shut down the bar, all of which failed. We were all 21, so he couldn't nail us on underage drinking. We had built it as a freestanding structure, so the bar had violated no official furniture or fire-code rules. We'd even attached the mirrors to the walls with poster putty.

The senior tutor's last resort was to stick us with an extra suite-mate, who was supposed to move into the room then occupied by the bar for the spring semester. Instead, Ben, the most altruistic of the four of us, gave up his own bedroom and moved his bed into the common room; the new suite-mate, Drew, became one of our bartenders; and the Mask and Spear was not dismantled until the day of our graduation. (We donated it to a group of rising seniors who re-opened it the following year and renamed it "The Mass Conspiracy.")[1]

A good bar should have some good house cocktails, and it was in the process of cocktail-recipe design that we started blind-tasting the top-shelf liquors against more humble brands. We soon discovered that we liked Smirnoff more than Absolut, although we resisted the temptation to refill our top-shelf bottles with the cheaper stuff; we felt it would be disrespectful to the bottle's patron.

However, there's anecdotal evidence that many bars—the kind that actually charge their customers—do just that, substituting mid-range liquors for top-shelf brands when they pour mixed drinks. And almost none of them get caught, because almost nobody can taste the difference.

The notion that expensive liquors might not taste any better than cheaper ones was exciting for college kids on a serious budget, and blind tasting became a popular sport in the Mask and Spear. However, I was the only one of the suite-mates for whom continuing to pour cheap alcoholic drinks from bottles wrapped in brown paper bags would turn out to be a career path.

Dan and I came up with the idea for *The Wine Trials* almost a decade later. Like an increasing number of Americans, we both enjoyed wine, but we had been increasingly put off by how opaque the process of buying wine has become.

Even in the midst of America's wine renaissance, there is a haze that surrounds the experience of the everyday wine buyer. Wine pricing seems more arbitrary, wine ratings less useful, and wine labeling more confusing than ever before. And more than ever, the wines most widely available in America—from Yellow Tail to Dom Pérignon—are being marketed with a method once reserved for fashion and cosmetics: by selling an image, a lifestyle, a social norm.

Consolidated wine companies, operating from the bottom end to the top end, have flooded the US market with new graphic savvy, introducing "critter wines" that have upended wine's traditional sense of hierarchy with wine packaging that seems designed to shock you, or at least to make you giggle. Over time, amateur wine enthusiasts learn to anticipate what a red Burgundy or a New Zealand Sauvignon Blanc is going to taste like, but how is *anyone* supposed to know what to expect from a wine called "Smoking Loon," "Fat Bastard," or "Bitch"?

Massive New World companies and their so-called "critter wines" have taken large swaths of wine shelves from the Old World incumbents through brute marketing force—helped along, perhaps, by the preference of wine magazine critics for the critter wines' generally bold, aggressive style. And production capacities of those companies are reaching unheard-of numbers. The Australian wine brand that really started the critter-wine revolution, Yellow Tail, has emerged in less than a decade as an unstoppable cheap-wine force, growing US sales from one million bottles per year in 2001 to more than 100 million bottles in 2006—one for every three US citizens.

None of this has made it any easier for consumers to walk into a store and buy a bottle of wine, nor has it simplified the process of choosing from a restaurant wine list. If anything, the American wine shelf is less orderly and more impenetrable than it was before the renaissance began. To compound this problem, Americans are increasingly buying wine at places like supermarkets, big-box stores, or chain restaurants where there's no wine counselor around to explain the differences between bottles.

In our attempts to fashion order from the chaos, we generally fall back on three basic criteria in choosing wine: price, ratings, and brand. Unfortunately, all of these criteria can be misleading.

We assume that the price of the wine will be correlated with our preferences—that if we want a better wine we'll have to spend a bit more money—but as our blind tastings of 6,000 glasses have shown, that's often not the case. The chapters that follow will reveal our surprising results: when you hide the label, most everyday wine drinkers actually prefer *cheaper* wine to more expensive wine.

We rely on the numerical ratings of wines in magazines like *Wine Spectator* and *Wine Advocate*, but these ratings display a consistently strong preference for expensive wines—a correlation that contrasts with our blind tasting results and with the scientific results of others in the field. This leaves everyday wine drinkers with little reason to assume that their tastes will agree with those of the magazine critics.

We also fall back, consciously or unconsciously, on brand—a wine's name, look, label, image, and advertisements we've seen—when making buying decisions. But every dollar of revenue that producers spend on marketing is a dollar less they're spending on making wine, so when you buy a bottle that's been well promoted, you're *less* likely to get a good value for your money, not more. Some of the world's most prestigious producers, like Château d'Yquem and Dom Pérignon, have now been acquired by luxury-goods manufacturers like Moët Hennessy Louis Vuitton, whose aim is to extract ever-increasing amounts of value from those famous brand names. The result is that behavioral lifestyle marketing has reached a crescendo.

Meanwhile, perceived shortages in supply, along with 95-to-100-point ratings of magazine critics, have driven the prices of some premium California wines and top Bordeaux wines through the roof—$5,000 per bottle or more, for example, for the 2005 release of Château Pétrus—and the industry seems to be in more desperate need of a reality check than ever before. This book will explore the possibility that everyday wine drinkers' enjoyment of expensive wines and famous brands may be the results of a placebo effect that is in part unrelated to the qualities of the wine itself.

There is a solution to all of these problems. I have come to believe that the best way to fashion order from the chaos of the wine shelf is by blind tasting. This book is the result of 17 blind wine tastings that we held around the US over the course of the past year. Our more than 500 blind tasters represented a mix of wine experts and everyday wine drinkers—including several former Mask and Spear patrons.

Once you're armed with gustatory information instead of marketing *mis*information, you will be better able to choose wines whose regions and styles correspond to what you actually like. Once you start blind tasting, you will be better able to develop a set of preferences that's uniquely yours, not guided by prices, magazine critics, or brands. That's not to say that you, too—if you're not already an expert—won't come to like expensive wine more as your knowledge of wine grows. But don't be too surprised if your preferences, even as they become more sophisticated, never turn out to match up well to the hierarchical structure that currently dominates the industry.

To get you started, the authors and editors, drawing on the evaluations of our 507 blind tasters, will recommend 100 widely available wines under $15 that experts and non-experts liked more in our tastings than bottles that cost $50 to $150.

This book is dedicated to the idea that blind tasting can help us stop spending too much money on wines we don't really like, and that it can help us start spending less money on wines we really do like. There are a lot of social, psychological, and informational obstacles blocking the way to that goal. Within these pages I will provide you with a map around those obstacles, a guide to developing trust in your own palate, and a short treatise on the ways that the modern market fails us when we outsource our taste to others.

Neither Dan nor I had any idea that our results would turn out to be this surprising. In retrospect, though, the truth had been staring us in the face since the days of the Mask and Spear.

Chapter 1 Blind taste

Dom Pérignon, a $150 Champagne from France, and Domaine Ste. Michelle Cuvée Brut, a $12 sparkling wine from Washington State, are both made in the traditional Champagne method. Both wines are widely available at wine stores, liquor stores, and many restaurants. Both are dry, with high acidity. The two bottles are more or less the same size and shape. So why are wine drinkers willing to pay more than 12 times more for one than for the other?

The most obvious explanation would be that, to most wine drinkers, the liquid inside the bottle of Dom Pérignon tastes better than the liquid inside the bottle of Domaine Ste. Michelle—if not 12 times better, then at least somewhat better.[2] However, that doesn't seem to be the case. When we served these two sparkling wines head-to-head in five different blind tastings, with the labels hidden inside brown paper bags, 41 of 62 tasters—about two thirds—preferred the Domaine Ste. Michelle.

This doesn't seem to be a single, idiosyncratic instance in which people's tastes happen to run contrary to popular wisdom or market prices. In a year-long series of blind tastings around the country in which we poured more than 6,000 glasses of wine from brown-bagged bottles that cost from $1.50 to $150, *people actually preferred the cheaper wines to the more expensive wines— by a statistically significant margin.*

Our 507 blind tasters represented many different segments of the wine-buying world. They were professionals in a wide range of fields. Some were wine experts, others everyday wine drinkers. They included New York City sommeliers and Harvard professors, winemakers from France, neuroscientists and artists, top chefs and college students, doctors and lawyers, wine importers and wine store owners, novelists and economists, TV comedy writers and oenologists, bartenders and grad students, 21-year-olds and 88-year-olds, socialists and conservatives, heavy drinkers and lightweights.

On the whole, tasters preferred a nine-dollar Beringer Founders' Estate Cabernet Sauvignon to a $120 wine from the same grape and the same producer: Beringer Private Reserve Cabernet Sauvignon. They preferred a six-dollar Vinho Verde from Portugal to a $40 Cakebread Chardonnay and a $50 Chassagne-Montrachet 1er Cru from Louis Latour. And when we concealed the labels and prices of 27 sparkling wines and asked people to rate them, the Dom Pérignon finished 17th—behind 14 sparkling wines that cost less than $15, eight of which cost less than $10.[3]

Does this mean that the $12 Domaine Ste. Michelle is *objectively better* than the $150 bottle of Dom? In an abstract, Platonic sense—or by established wine industry norms—probably not. In fact, the wine experts among our tasters didn't dislike the expensive wines in the way that everyday wine drinkers did; they liked more expensive wines as much, or even a bit more, than cheaper wines.

But the vast majority of wine consumers are everyday wine drinkers, not experts. At a minimum, it seems clear that many Americans might be wasting at least $138 when they buy Dom Pérignon for special occasions.

There is a mounting body of evidence from within and without the wine world that wine pricing is more arbitrary than one might assume, but ours was one of the first studies to show an *inverse* correlation between price and preference. That inverse correlation was moderate but statistically significant across all of our tasters ($p=0.038$; this means that there was only a 3.8% probability that our results came about by chance—in the sciences, the generally accepted standard for statistical significance is a p-value of less than 5%). When you exclude the very cheapest and most expensive wines and just look at the mid-range wines—those priced between $6 and $15—the effect is even stronger ($p=0.004$).

We did not allow the tasters to discuss the wines with each other before rating them, and we kept the wines concealed in their numbered brown paper bags until after the evaluation forms had been turned in. In order to weigh the results of consistent tasters more than inconsistent tasters, we subjected people to the "twin-wine test," serving them two identical wines in the same flight of six—unbeknownst to the tasters, of course. With the help of our statistics team, we gave less weight to the opinions of tasters who rated the identical wines differently.

The design of our large-scale experiment is explained in more detail in appendix 1, written by statisticians Jake Katz and Jay Emerson. The results are explained in technical form in Appendix 2, written by economists Johan Almenberg and Anna Dreber Almenberg, and they're also presented in an academic paper that you can download at the American Association of Wine Economists website, the Stockholm School of Economics website, and at our own website.[4]

By no means are all wine critics and commentators in denial of this effect. Many have commented on the arbitrariness of pricing, including Master of Wine Jancis Robinson, one of the world's foremost wine writers, who has observed a "lack of correlation between price and pleasure." She writes: "Perhaps it is not so surprising that a first-rate example of a little-known wine can seem much more memorable than something more famous selling at ten times the price...What is more extraordinary is the wild price variation at the very top end. Demand bubbles up mysteriously, apparently fuelled by fashion and rumour as much as by intrinsic quality."[5]

In their seminal 1976 book on wine quality measurement, *Wines: Their Sensory Evaluation*, UC Davis professors Maynard Amerine (an oenologist) and Edward Roessler (a mathematician) tend to concur, although they, like Robinson, focus on the overpricing of superpremium wines: "[P]rice depends on many factors that are not necessarily related to quality. Those who buy wines on a price basis deserve what they get. ... Some famous vineyards, secure in the knowledge that they have an established market, often charge whatever the market will bear."[6]

Between 1997 and 2001, researchers Sébastien Lecocq and Michael Visser conducted three large-scale expert blind tastings of a total of 1,409 wines from Bordeaux and Burgundy under highly controlled conditions with professional French tasters from the Institut National de la Consommation. They found that the tasters' sensory evaluations of the wines were only very weakly correlated with price, leading Lecocq and Visser to conclude that "the market price of Bordeaux wine can be explained primarily by the objective characteristics appearing on the label of the bottle." Lecocq and Visser's tastings involved only experts, but they foreshadow our results with everyday wine drinkers when they suggest that "when non-experts blind-taste cheap and expensive wines they typically tend to prefer the cheaper ones."[7]

In a series of blind tastings conducted by Hilke Plassmann, Antonio Rangel, and their colleagues at Stanford Business School and Cal Tech—part of an important brain-scanning study that I'll come back to in chapter 2—everyday wine drinkers rated the cheap wines *higher* than they rated the expensive wines, just as they did in our blind tastings. And in an experiment conducted by Roman Weil, which will be discussed in chapter 3, everyday wine drinkers didn't prefer reserve wines to regular wines, even though the wines differed in price by an order of magnitude.

Our observations, like those of the scholars above, could hardly contrast any more starkly with the patterns of wine ratings on the 100-point scales used by magazine critics, which tend to track wine prices consistently.

What is going on here? If blind tasting experiments show that wine pricing is arbitrary from the perspective of everyday wine drinkers, then why are the magazine ratings that they rely on so correlated with price? And why do everyday wine drinkers ever spend money on expensive wine?

Chapter 2 The taste of money

Moët & Chandon, the producer of Dom Pérignon, sells more than 60 million bottles of premium-priced Champagne every year—most of them to everyday wine drinkers, not wine professionals. Putting aside our results for a moment, it's hard to imagine that millions of consumers would be buying $30 to $150 Champagnes and really, truly enjoying them less than $10 sparkling wines. Most of those people must *feel*, at least, that they're getting their money's worth; otherwise, presumably, they wouldn't keep buying expensive Champagne.[8]

The sheer number of amateur wine bloggers on the Internet at the moment, many of whom spend hours every day writing extensive reviews for no pay, seems evidence enough to demonstrate wine lovers' passionate enjoyment of expensive wine. It would seem ludicrous to suggest that amateur wine lovers are not really enjoying their $2,000 bottles of Château Margaux or Screaming Eagle, or to suspect their passion to be anything less than genuine. Yet even that passion seems to conflict with our results—and with the results of scientists in wine economics and cognition.

What do we make, for instance, of the work of wine researcher Fréderic Brochet, who fooled 57 French wine experts by serving them two identical wines, one in an expensive Grand Cru bottle, the other in a cheap Vin de Table bottle? Although both bottles contained the same wine—a mid-range Bordeaux—Brochet's subjects preferred the wine from the Grand Cru bottle by a dramatic margin. They used positive terms like "excellent," "good," "complex," and "long" more than twice as often when describing the supposed Grand Cru as they did when describing the supposed Vin de Table, and, conversely, used negative terms like "unbalanced," "short," "flat," and "simple" more than twice as much when describing the supposed Vin de Table.

Another of Brochet's experiments showed that, like price, the color of a wine can affect subjects' reported experiences. When 54 subjects tasted a white wine under normal conditions, they tended to use typical white-wine descriptors (e.g. "fresh," "lemon," "apricot," and "honey") to describe their experience. But when they tasted that same white wine when it had been colored with a flavorless dye to look like red wine, the tasters switched to typical red-wine descriptors (e.g. "red currant," "cherry," "raspberry," and "spice"). The influence of the wine's color on their taste experience, or at least their judgment, was profound.[9]

Coming back to *Wines: Their Sensory Evaluation*, Amerine and Roessler anticipate Brochet's results in that book: "It is surprising," they write, "how many so-called wine experts are 'label drinkers.' Their sensory judgment is based on the source or reputation of the wine, or its producer, or the year of production."

But what do they mean by "sensory judgment"? Is it wine drinkers' *judgment* of the experience that's altered by the knowledge that a wine is expensive, or is it the *experience itself*?

I believe it to be the latter: it's the experience itself that changes when you know the wine is expensive. I do not believe that most wine drinkers simply pretend to like wine better because it's expensive, and I do not believe that they are lying to others, or even to themselves, when they report getting more pleasure from premium-priced wine.

I believe that wine actually tastes better when you know it's expensive, in every meaningful sense of the word "taste." For wine as for medicine, the placebo effect is not a mere delusion; it is a physical reality. The experience of sipping a wine you know to be expensive, then, is a real taste experience. It is the taste of money.

The best evidence that the placebo effect can change the experience of drinking itself comes from an article co-authored by a member of our Scientific Advisory Board, Shane Frederick of MIT's Sloan School of Management, along with his MIT colleague Dan Ariely, author of the new book *Predictably Irrational*, and Leonard Lee of Columbia Business School. It's an article about beer.

An interesting study done in 1964 showed that beer drinkers, under experimental conditions, didn't prefer their favorite beers in blind tastings when the labels were hidden.[10] But Frederick and his colleagues ran a more complex experiment that involved adding balsamic vinegar to some of the beer before serving it.

Here's how it worked: 388 tasters were randomly assigned to three different groups. The first group of tasters rated both beers—with and without vinegar—with no information about the ingredients, and 59% of them preferred the beer with vinegar (apparently, for many people, balsamic vinegar can improve the taste of beer). Tasters in the second group were instead informed of the ingredients before tasting; of that group, only 30% preferred the beer with vinegar. Their negative expectations seem to have colored their experience and reduced the pleasure they got from drinking the vinegared beer. Most interesting, however, were the tasters in the third group, who were told about the vinegar *after* tasting it, but *before* rating it. That group, like the first group, preferred the vinegared beer—even though they knew it contained vinegar before assigning their ratings. The first and third groups did not differ significantly in their preferences.[11]

The punch line is that the knowledge that there was vinegar in the beer affected people's *taste experience* if they were told about it beforehand, but it didn't significantly change their *judgment* of the beer after they'd already tasted. To me, this is strong evidence that expectations exert more influence on the level of taste *experience* than they do on the level of taste *judgment*.

In January 2008, Hilke Plassmann, Antonio Rangel, and their colleagues at Stanford Business School and the California Institute of Technology published an article in the *Proceedings of the National Academy of Sciences* that added a set of fMRI brain-scan results to this remarkable body of evidence.[12] fMRI—short for functional magnetic resonance imaging—is a brain-scanning technology that (roughly speaking) measures changes in blood flow to different parts of the brain over time. There are some major drawbacks to the technique; for instance, subjects must lie very still inside a cylinder, which is obviously a bit different from the way we normally enjoy wine. More importantly, subjects in fMRI experiments have to sip liquids from a tube—so they don't get to swirl and smell the wine.

Still, Plassmann and Rangel's results are fascinating. In their experiment, 20 subjects in fMRI machines were told that they would taste five different Cabernet Sauvignon wines whose retail prices were $5, $10, $35, $45, and $90. In reality, the subjects were only served three wines: a $5 wine, a $35 wine, and a $90 wine. They were served the $5 wine twice, once while being told it cost $45 and once while being told its real cost. Likewise, they were served the $90 wine twice, once while being told it cost $10.

If you've read up to this point in the book, you probably won't be surprised by what happened: subjects' preferences correlated with the *fake* prices of the wines, not with the *actual* prices. When people thought they were drinking $90 wine, they loved it, even if it was actually $10 wine. What's more, blood flow to a brain area commonly associated with pleasure—the left medial orbitofrontal cortex—also was correlated with the fake price of the wines, but not with the actual price. For the first time, the neural correlates of price expectations *creating* pleasure were visible.

In a little-reported footnote to their study, Plassmann and Rangel had their subjects taste the same wines a few weeks later during a "post-experimental session without price cues"—that is, a straight-up blind tasting. And in that tasting, subjects actually preferred the $5 wine to the $90 wine. Sound familiar?

The wine placebo effect is real. We must accept that truth about ourselves. It doesn't mean that wine aficionados and experts are con artists, nor does it mean that people don't legitimately sense pleasurable qualities in very expensive wine, even when they taste it blind. But it does mean that when we don't taste blind, it's almost impossible to know whether the pleasure of expensive wine is coming from its own taste, or from the taste of money.

Chapter 3 The perfect palate?

At press time, *Wine Spectator* had rated 6,475 wines from the 2000 to 2007 vintages that cost $10 or less. Of those, only three of them—four hundredths of one percent—scored above 90 on the magazine's 100-point scale, and none scored above 91. By comparison, for those same vintages, of the 2,490 wines reviewed in *Wine Spectator* that cost $100 or more, 1,781 of them—more than 71%—scored above 90. *Wine Enthusiast* tells a similar story: of the 5,896 wines from the 2000 to 2007 vintages listed at $10 or less in their database, only two scored above 91.[13]

Taste and smell, the so-called "chemical senses," are the most fickle and least quantifiable of our bodies' sensory systems, and wine is one of the most volatile substances that we regularly ingest. When people rate tastes and smells, the variance in their results tends to be extraordinarily high, even in the most predictable and controlled cognitive tests.

Considering wine's high sensitivity to oxygen, to temperature, and to time—complicated further by the physical unpredictability of our palates—the degree of correlation between price and qualitative score in the mainstream wine publications has become harder and harder to swallow with each additional scientific study that's been published on the subject. How could our results diverge so dramatically from the magazine critics' opinions?

Putting aside, for a moment, the implausibility of the notion that *Wine Spectator*'s price-score correlation could have occurred naturally under controlled blind tasting conditions, the most obvious explanation for this disconnect would be that expensive wine is simply an acquired taste, and that the vast majority of wine drinkers—like the subjects of the experiments cited above, including ours—just haven't acquired that taste the way that these magazines' elite tasters have. Perhaps the magazines have cornered the market on critics who have "perfect palates"—the rare ability to taste something totally different in these expensive wines, something that simply *could not exist* in a $10 bottle. Maybe it's something that amateur wine drinkers, and even many wine experts, just can't detect, or—alternatively—can detect, but dislike.

In a fascinating study by Roman Weil, non-experts were given blind tastes of the same wine from two different vintages, one deemed "good" by wine experts, the other deemed "bad." Tasters also compared a prestigious reserve bottling against a regular bottling, again blind. In both cases, the tasters didn't do much better than chance at telling the two wines apart, and even when they did, they were as likely to prefer the cheap bottle as the expensive bottle—even though, in both cases, the prices differed by an order of magnitude.[14]

Weil did not administer his test to wine experts, but there is evidence that experts and everyday wine drinkers do have different taste in wine. Within the subset of wine experts in our blind tastings, there was a slight *positive* correlation—rather than a negative one—between price and preference. Still, the effect was only marginally significant, and our experts' opinions were nowhere near as price-correlated as are the *Wine Spectator* critics'. Neither were the opinions of Lecocq and Visser's wine experts. In fact, to my knowledge, no scientific blind-tasting study of wine experts has ever shown expensive wines to do as consistently well, or cheap wines to do as consistently poorly, as they do in *Wine Spectator*.

On the other hand, if the critics *weren't* tasting blind, the discrepancy between their strong price-rating correlations and our blind tasting results would suddenly make a lot more sense: the wine placebo effect could be guiding these critics to consistently overrate the expensive wines.

Before I go any further, let me be clear that the points I'm making in this chapter refer largely to wine magazines: *Wine*

Spectator, Robert Parker's *Wine Advocate*, *Wine Enthusiast*, and so on. There are numerous great wine critics and writers out there—many of whom write for newspapers, or who maintain wine blogs—to whom this critique does not apply. Some critics *do* taste blind, and many don't use numerical ratings for wines. However, in the modern wine industry, Robert Parker and *Wine Spectator*—perhaps in part becaues of the mere fact that they *do* assign 100-point ratings—exert a more powerful influence over the industry, and over price trends, than do the other critics.

Do the magazine critics taste blind? Well, the father of the US wine-magazine industry and inventor of the 100-point rating scale, for one, doesn't: Robert Parker freely admits that he sometimes rates wine based on non-blind tasting.

Interestingly, though, *Wine Spectator*, whose high scores appear to be even more closely correlated with high prices than Parker's, makes almost as big a deal about blind tasting as I do. James Laube, one of *Spectator*'s senior editors, has gone so far as to write a blog article about the importance of blind tasting. "*Wine Spectator* has always believed in blind tastings," Laube explains. "In practice, that means that tasters review wines in coherent flights, to give context. We know the region, the vintage and the grape variety, if relevant. But we don't know the producer or the price."[15]

Consider that statement for a moment: the magazine critics are tasting blind, but they know the region, the vintage, and the grape variety. Let's say it's a red wine, the appellation is Hermitage,[16] and the vintage is 2005. The cheapest possible wine in the *Spectator* database that would fit those criteria costs $49. And, to their credit, the *Spectator* tasters certainly know enough about wine to know that Hermitage reds are going to be expensive. In that example, then, they *would* know the price, or at least the price category, before tasting—which means that they wouldn't really be tasting blind. They'd know that they were tasting expensive wines, and they'd have full frontal exposure to the wine placebo effect.

At least Laube admits that his staff is only human. "Even the professionals 'miss' a wine now and then," writes Laube, "the same way the refs miss a call. But we believe that if we can eliminate any possibility of bias, we're at least giving you a fair and honest assessment of the wines." Luckily for Laube, it seems that his team of professionals hasn't "missed a call" and accidentally scored a wine under $10 above 91 in at least the past 6,475 tries.

One of the more compelling scenes in the 2004 documentary film *Mondovino* depicts fashion-empire heir and wine producer Salvatore Ferragamo hanging out with James Suckling, the *Wine Spectator* critic who rates Ferragamo's wine for the magazine. If you haven't seen *Mondovino*, it's worth it just to check out this priceless little scene, which seems like it's straight out of *Borat*: that is, the joke's on Suckling, but he doesn't seem to know it.

Suckling seems to fancy himself a sort of ambassador for Italian wine in the modern era: "Italian wine is the wine of our generation," says Suckling. "Our parents drank French wines, wore Hèrmes, went to Paris. Our generation, we wear Armani, Ferragamo...Prada, and then we drink Italian wines, eat Italian food, and travel to Florence, Rome, Venice." Talking about the 90 he's awarded to Ferragamo's wine, Suckling says: "I was generous, I thought. But he is my landlord." Then the two joke about the idea of renegotiating Suckling's rent for a 95.

None of the evidence in *Mondovino*—or anywhere else—is quite sufficient to prove that there's any actual corruption going on. Suckling and Ferragamo, of course, are just joking around when they talk about paying for high ratings. And it's not quite *impossible*—just statistically improbable—that *Spectator* critics are among the only people on Earth with perfect palates.

But what kind of message does it send that the magazine continues to accept and publish full-page advertisements for many of the same wines it's reviewing and scoring? And what kind of message does it send to everyday wine drinkers that Suckling—and, by extension, *Wine Spectator*—openly flaunts a buddy-buddy relationship with the producer whose wines he's scoring?

It is particularly fitting, I think, that Suckling should be hanging out with a fashion maven, of all people. Because, as I will suggest in the next chapter, the wine industry and its magazine critics are looking more like fashionistas every day.

And in the end, corrupt or not corrupt, placebo effects or perfect palates, the problem is the same: if magazine critics' results have so little in common with the palates of everyday wine drinkers, then why would everyday wine drinkers expect that they'd be any more likely to enjoy a 95-point wine than an 80-point wine? Why, for that matter, should everyday wine drinkers pay any attention at all to those numerical ratings?

Chapter 4 Dom Pérignon's new clothes

As I've shown thus far, human beings are pretty suggestible when it comes to wine. The magazine critics are suggesting that we should like expensive wine more than cheap wine; and when we know it's expensive or highly rated, we actually *do* like it more—our brains' pleasure areas even light up on brain scans. The high prices of prestigious wines have started the engine of the placebo effect, and the magazine critics' endorsement of the price-quality relationship has added fuel. But even if we like it more, there is another component that goes into our choice to spend *so much* more for expensive wine: the desire to be seen owning and drinking it.

It often seems that the act of buying, serving, and drinking expensive wine is, beyond the mere sensory experience, a way for people to display their wealth to other people—a form of conspicuous consumption. I think of it as an *aspirational* act: behavior driven by the aspiration to be part of the next higher social class, a symbol of a more expensive way of life. As such, conspicuous consumption is actually more associated with the new-money middle class than with the old-money upper class; members of the upper class tend to be less brand-driven, or at least more discreet, with their spending. That's why you see more Ferraris in Miami than you do in Modena, where they're made.

By no means is every oenophile an aspirational conspicuous consumer. But the habit of displaying empty bottles of wine from prestigious producers and vintages in strategic locations around one's house, at least, would point toward the conspicuous-consumption theory of premium wine pricing. While some people do keep and display bottles they've enjoyed for merely nostalgic purposes, it would seem too much for coincidence that they so often happen to be only the expensive bottles. (On the other hand, the enjoyment of those expensive bottles could be traced back to the placebo effect, too.)

The most extreme case of conspicuous wine consumption I've seen was at Nikki Beach, a fashionable restaurant-lounge in Saint-Tropez on the French Riviera. Most tables, including mine, were drinking refreshing rosé from the nearby Côtes de Provence region—possibly the perfect seaside wine. Some tables had ordered Champagne, though, which was marked up spectacularly.

One table of Kuwaitis nearby had ordered several magnums of Cristal, one of the world's most expensive Champagnes—it comes in crystal bottles—for thousands of dollars each. They were spraying each other with the Champagne, and a couple of them were drenched, but strangely, their glasses were completely dry. When I asked a waiter why the Kuwaitis weren't actually *drinking* the Cristal, he told me that the custom of spraying but not drinking was something he'd often seen among rich Arab customers at Nikki Beach: it was against their religion to consume alcohol.

Of course, that kind of self-conscious conspicuous consumption is the exception to the rule. Few people would be as open as those Kuwaitis were about being conspicuous wine consumers. But I think that this can be attributed to an honest mistake: the wine placebo effect prevents people from *realizing* that they're conspicuous consumers. When the placebo effect works, *it actually makes the wine taste good*, thus making its purchase feel more like a justified exchange of goods at fair market value than an act of conspicuous consumption. It rarely *feels* as though you've really paid more for the bottle, label, and marketing than you've paid for the liquid within. That's why some producers are able to get away with selling premium wines at a markup that would seem insane from any cost-of-production perspective.

Nowhere is that markup more insane than in the world of sparkling wines. This might be true in part because sparkling wines are probably the most difficult of all wine categories to blind taste and compare; carbon dioxide does a pretty good job of obscuring the differences between them. When you taste sparkling wines, it's a lot easier to detect differences on the nose than on the mouth; once the bubbles hit your tongue, your ability to sense much beyond sweetness or dryness is significantly stunted.

Try this experiment: taste a couple of sparkling wines just after opening them, and jot down your notes. Then, leave the wines out and open until their fizz disappears. When you taste them again, not only will the wines have changed, they'll also seem much more different from each other than they did initially. Their acidity and oakiness, if any, will become more pronounced, and you'll detect more fruit flavors on the palate.

That's a secret that the premium Champagne producers don't want to let out. From their perspective, Champagne's status as a celebratory, special-occasion wine that represents the idea that no expense was spared, whether at a glamorous New Year's Eve party or a wedding, makes it a fertile ground for premium markups on unremarkable wines—wines that, in other circumstances, might not be demonstrably better than much cheaper wines.

Our blind tasters sampled more than 350 glasses of 27 sparkling wines, of which eight under $15 qualified for our top 100. All eight of these, including the $8 Segura Viudas Brut and the $9 Freixenet Cordon Negro Brut, beat both Dom Pérignon and Veuve Clicquot in our tastings. And as I mentioned in chapter 1, when the wines were tasted against each other, 41 of 62 tasters—about two thirds—preferred a $12 Domaine Ste. Michelle Brut from Washington State to a $150 Dom Pérignon.

The placebo effect aside, why shouldn't Dom Pérignon—given its popularity with everyday wine drinkers, not just experts—do better, at least, than *that*?

A peek at www.lvmh.com—the website of Moët Hennessy Louis Vuitton, owner of both Veuve Clicquot and Moët & Chandon, producer of Dom Pérignon—might offer a clue. Aside from Champagne and those famously imitated handbags, the LVMH portfolio is a roll call of the world's aspirational luxury lifestyle brands: Acqua di Parma, Belvedere and Chopin vodka, Christian Dior perfume and watches, Château d'Yquem wine, Fendi, Givenchy, Guerlain, Kenzo, Krug, Marc Jacobs, Sephora, TAG Heuer, and so on.

The company also runs the consumer branch of De Beers, the diamond empire, and—surprise, surprise—a vast network of duty-free shops at airports around the world. LVMH, which recorded 2007 revenues of $26 billion—by comparison, Google's revenues were less than half that—is probably the world's most successful practitioner of selling conspicuous consumption. In a year that saw the worldwide economy suffer, LVMH had its best year ever.

But how much is the company actually spending on *making* Champagne? Well, they don't make that exact information public, but in 2007, LVMH reported that only 35% of revenues went toward the cost of goods, while 43%—that's $11 billion—went to the cost of sales, marketing, and overhead.[17] In contrast, Constellation Brands, the monster wine conglomerate in the US mass-market wine world, reported in its 2007 annual report that, on the cost side, 58% of revenues went toward the cost of goods, while Constellation spent just 12% of revenues on the cost of sales, marketing, and overhead:[18]

Company	2007 revenues	Cost of goods	Sales, marketing, and overhead
LVMH	$26 billion	$9 billion (35% of revenues)	$11 billion (43% of revenues)
Constellation	$6.4 billion	$3.7 billion (58% of revenues)	$768 million (12% of revenues)

It's starting to look less surprising that the liquid inside Dom Pérignon might not taste so much better than the liquid inside a much cheaper bottle: we're paying our portion of glossy advertisements, corporate sponsorships, armies of top-tier MBAs in fantastic offices, parties at the world's most exclusive nightclubs, and a payroll that includes Tiger Woods, Claudia Schiffer, Catherine Deneuve, André Agassi, Steffi Graf, and Mikhail Gorbachev (who has come a long way since his work leading a communist country). And they publicly flaunt that payroll. Why do we fall for it?

Well, flip through LVMH's 2007 annual report, and you'll discover that the company seems to have found the consumer-products-industry holy grail: a rare phenomenon known in economics as a Veblen good. Normal microeconomic theory predicts that the demand for a good decreases when the price goes up, but Veblen goods—named for the social theorist Thorstein Veblen, author of *The Theory of the Leisure Class*—are things that people actually want *more* when the price is raised.

Justin Weinberg, a philosopher at the University of South Carolina, has suggested that expensive wines often function as Veblen goods—that a wine's high price alone can be "sufficient to stimulate a strong interest in consuming it."[19] In the case of premium-priced Champagne, the more it costs, the more impressive it is—even to ourselves. In some cases, the pleasure we're getting from the expensive bottle might even have virtually nothing to do with what's inside, and everything to do with the label, the image, and simply the price we've paid.

That language might sound familiar to the authors of the LVMH annual report, who boasted that over the past year, "the [Champagne] brand continued its very strong international media presence through the 'Be Fabulous' promotional campaign. ... The Wines and Spirits business group recorded organic revenue growth of 13%, driven by the increase in volumes…and the implementation of a policy to raise prices." The report continues: "the Moët Hennessy distribution network applied the planned price increases, thus strengthening its premium positioning."

Increase the price of Champagne to *strengthen* positioning?

LVMH seems to know they've got a Veblen good on their hands, and they can barely contain the enthusiasm (within the constraints of sedate Wall Street lingo, anyway) to convey that point to their shareholders. But they also seem to know that they can only continue to pull it off if they keep marketing their wine like a perfume, a diamond ring, a leather bag, or a Swiss watch, which means keeping Woods, Schiffer, and Gorbachev on board, too.

At some point, the annual report moves on to Cognac, un-ironically describing the "major promotional plans" that "enhanced and intensified the dynamic image of the brand," telling of "an advertising campaign...titled Flaunt Your Taste," which "gave Hennessy high visibility and an enhanced image of sophistication."

"Flaunt Your Taste."

Veblen couldn't have put it any better had he lived today.

What saves fashion mavens from the deepest sort of ridicule is that they don't take themselves too seriously. They seem to know how arbitrary their tastemaking is, and understand the arbitrariness of declaring one dress to be worth $10,000 and another to be worth $50. There's a certain tongue-in-cheek aspect to their attitude; they embrace the ridiculousness of their expert opinions.

As such, to lodge an exposé of the fashion industry's lack of substance would be beside the point—an argument against a straw man. I doubt that anybody who spends $10,000 on a dress is under the delusion that it's 2,000 times more attractive than something they could get at H&M.

Rather, the fashionistas revel in the absurdity of the expenditure, at peace with the arbitrariness of any given trend-of-the-moment anointment. They seem comfortable with their decision not to rate fashion styles blind, comfortable with the idea that who's wearing something is as important, or more important, than what's being worn, and comfortable with the idea that it's probably something that will go out of fashion next year, and come back into fashion three decades hence. The fashion world is the very definition of self-conscious conspicuous consumption. It is what it is, and it knows what it is.

I believe that wine can be, and should be, something more substantive than that. There's something more personal about putting something *inside* your body than putting something *on* your body, and since the days of Plato and Aristotle, the idea has been floating around that something more rigorous, scientific, and philosophical can emerge from the enterprise of creating, tasting, and thinking about wine. It was that sentiment that led Alexandre Dumas to famously dub wine the "intellectual part" of the meal.

But when you consider the fact that rigorous blind tasting is still the exception in the world of wine ratings, and fuzzy, placebo-effect-driven, conspicuous-consumption-clouded wine talk the rule, we wine enthusiasts start to look a lot like those Kuwaitis at Nikki Beach, spraying each other with obscure fruit adjectives, futures prices, and 100-point scores.

And unlike those guys, we don't generally get supermodels coming over to sit down with us unsolicited.

Chapter 5 So what?

Is there anything really wrong with this whole picture? Some interpreters of the body of evidence I've presented in this book have suggested that the enjoyment of the wine placebo effect and conspicuous consumption are forms of consumer welfare that should be welcomed, not questioned. Their idea is that when you buy a product, you're not just acquiring its physical usefulness; you're also purchasing what economists might call the "social utility" of being associated with the brand. You're buying into a perceived lifestyle, and it makes you happy. In postwar America, among the foremost practitioners of lifestyle marketing have been the clothing, jewelry, liquor, glassware, higher education, tobacco, cosmetics, loudspeaker, and automotive industries.

"Conspicuous consumption and waste are an important part of social display," observes the *Economist* in an article about Plassmann and Rangel's work. "Deployed properly, they bring the rewards of status and better mating opportunities. For this to work, though, it helps if the displaying individual really believes that what he is buying is not only more expensive than the alternative, but better, too. Truly enjoying something simply because it is exclusive thus makes evolutionary sense."[20]

Moving on to the practical implications for the business world, the *Economist* then points out that "Rangel's research also has implications for retailers, marketing firms and luxury-goods producers. It suggests that a successful marketing campaign can not only make people more interested in a product, but also, truly, make them enjoy it more."

Although the article does not specifically suggest that this would justify those marketing campaigns' value to the economy, the implication seems to be there. That is, it wouldn't be much of a stretch to conclude that people's greater physical enjoyment of expensive goods once they know they're expensive *justifies*, from an economic standpoint, their high buy-in costs—and, by implication, their high marketing expenditures.

The fact that people like prestigious wine, in other words, means that the money that's been spent marketing its prestige has been spent *well*. It means that consumers benefit from all those good, expensive feelings exactly as they should, and nobody loses in the process. If $150 of pleasure is created by the combination of a marketing campaign and the $150 price tag itself, why should we mind? Can't we just dismiss this as a happy, if irrational, corner of the free market working properly?

Not in my view. In the case of wine, when price alone can convince people that a wine is good, winemakers lose their incentive to make wines that people would like if they were blind tasting—wines with *intrinsically* appealing qualities. What's worse, people start forgetting to pay attention to the differences between wines, because all the wine starts to taste the same.

And for all the fuss made about the boom in US wine consumption, that's what's happening right now. Giant wine conglomerates, many of them based in California and Australia— and there is more consolidation every year—are realizing that their money is better spent on billboards, banner ads, and magazine critics' junkets than on making wine.

When wineries compete to make better-tasting wines, the consumer wins, because over time, it raises the bar of quality for the wine industry. Substantive competition raises the quality of *all* wines. It encourages bad wineries to improve their quality, for instance, by spending more money on tasting and chemical analysis, or by modernizing their facilities.

But when wineries compete merely to market their wines more successfully, the consumer loses, because more of the wines' costs go toward marketing, and less toward winemaking. A great winemaker is your friend, but one that substitutes marketing for winemaking is the enemy of the wine consumer. And a company that spends as much (or more) money on marketing as it does on research, development, and production—a company like LVMH—is delivering poor value to consumers. When we pay their premiums and fund their advertising campaigns, we are literally *paying them to tell us that we like their product.* Why do we fall for it, again and again? Why do we transfer our social insecurities, in monetary form, to big companies?

Marketing wasn't always about appealing to our social or emotional insecurities, and it wasn't always a waste of resources. Look at any pre-World War II magazine, and you'll see pages full of advertisements that actually discussed the substantive advantages of their products. For instance, a pair of shoes or a shirt would be advertised as having more durable soles or fabric. That sort of advertising served an *informational* purpose: it informed the consumer about the product's availability and about the real differences between that product and others. It cast the product onto the consumer's radar screen, and the dissemination of that information helped the free market to function fluidly.

That's not what's going on when you see a wine associated with a scantily clad woman, a celebrity, or a kangaroo, or branded with a name like "Mommy's Time Out," "Four Emus," "Little Black Dress," or "Old Fart." What do these names have to do with wine? The information dissemination has been replaced by brands elbowing for emotional space in consumers' minds. Effective modern wine marketing is rarely about communicating the way the wine tastes or smells—it's more about communicating a lifestyle. It's about preying on our social needs—the same needs that drive our tendency toward conspicuous consumption—rather than our sensory ones.

In economic terms, I view the marketing of consumer products in the modern world as a zero-sum game. Every time a consumer chooses one sparkling wine over another based on marketing, and not on the results of blind tastings, the zero-sum game is played out. One company wins and another loses, but the money that both have spent competing on lifestyle marketing is wasted. For every winner, there's a loser, and there's no net benefit to consumers, or to the economy.

The emergence of emotional marketing, and the accompanying replacement of true consumer choice with an opaque network of intermediaries and social forces, is hardly limited to the wine industry. Take cars, for instance. Although the auto manufacturers, for the first time in a long while, are finally starting to market the fuel efficiency of their cars, the current Cadillac campaign is still more typical of the industry, at least in America: it emphasizes a zooming lifestyle and beautiful people, and it contains little or no discussion of the merits of the product itself.

Cadillac is an interesting study in modern marketing: on the verge of obsolescence, the company managed to reposition its image completely, from Eldorado to Escalade, turning itself from the canonical conspicuous-consumption emblem of Morty Seinfeld's generation into the canonical conspicuous-consumption emblem of Jay-Z's generation. Cadillac's new motto, scrawled across its glossy magazine ads, is simply this: "Life, liberty, and the pursuit."

Veblen would love it: "of happiness" has been cut from that famous Declaration of Independence phrase—a phrase that has, for generations, been understood to embody the essence of the American spirit. Happiness, it seems, is no longer the point. It's just "the pursuit."

The pursuit of *what*?

Blind tasting is not a one-sided issue. There has been some sophisticated discussion about its pros and cons. *New York Times* wine critic Eric Asimov, in an interesting pair of articles that engendered a lively debate on his blog, "The Pour," has argued that blind tasting is insufficient as a way to judge wine. "Blind tastings eliminate knowledge and context that can be significant in judging a wine...I feel it's a little like judging a book by reading one chapter or one page."[21] Insisting on blind tasting—continues Asimov in his second post on the subject—prevents you from understanding the wine you're judging: "It's almost an anti-intellectual position. Obviously what's in the glass matters. But I think the more knowledge you can bring to a wine, the better your understanding of that wine will be."[22]

Asimov makes a good point: that knowing a few things about a wine you're drinking really can enhance your experience of it. The intellectual enterprise of wine appreciation that Dumas described would certainly be incomplete without knowing what wine one is thinking or talking about. In fact, taking Asimov's point a step further, it would seem reasonable that knowing a wine's region, vintage, grapes, and history could even *make a wine taste better* in the same way that knowledge about price does—especially for someone who already knows a bit about wine. As such, I would not argue that you should brown-bag the wine that you serve with dinner. In fact, if the wine is expensive, telling everyone how much it cost you—though gauche—might even help your guests enjoy it more.

Nor would I suggest that descriptive reviews of wines should have to rely solely on blind tasting notes. Indeed, ours don't; they discuss grape varieties, and they even include critiques of bottle design. If a magazine lovingly describes the rolling hills of Tuscany in its review of a Tuscan wine, that's fair enough; the review creates a set of evocative images that might well enhance our experience of drinking the wine.

But none of this implies that it's appropriate for information that is universally acknowledged to create bias to be disclosed when you're *ranking or rating wines against each other.* If a magazine's tasters, just before assigning an evaluative score to that wine on a 100-point scale—a score that is likely to have a major impact on the wine's price, on its availability to everyday wine drinkers, and on the producer's financial well-being—are told that the wine they're about to taste is a 2005 Pomerol, or (on the other end of the spectrum) a wine from Baja California, the system falls apart.

In that case, the placebo effect—which, as Brochet and Weil have shown, applies to experts just as it does to everyday wine drinkers—colors the evaluation: good wines from inexpensive, little-known regions are penalized; average wines from famous, expensive regions are rewarded; and the chronic overrating and overpricing of prestige wines is perpetuated. This is the vicious cycle of non-blind rating that has poisoned the modern wine industry. It is the cycle that has driven the release price of a good vintage of Pétrus to $5,000 per bottle, and the cycle that maintains the price of Dom Pérignon at $150.

Wines should not always be *experienced* blind. But I believe that they should always be *judged* blind. Only if we begin assessing value *without any information at all* will the vast pricing discrepancies that have infiltrated the industry begin to right themselves over time.

As things stand, our society of wine drinkers—and consumers of other goods—rides on the placebo effect more than most people are willing to admit. My hope is that once you've begun tasting blind, the placebo effect will fade in favor of something better: the pleasure of enjoying a good wine at a good price—and a wine that you know is good, however little you might have paid. Once you're choosing wine purely on its merits, you've taken away the industry's power of lifestyle marketing, and you've enhanced your ability to find pleasure in an inexpensive bottle. You've become a real consumer.

And although advertisements would have you believe otherwise, the choice to buy a wine—or to buy anything else—on the reputation of a brand alone is a *sacrifice* of your individuality, not an expression of it. America is the country that spread free-market capitalism around the world, yet by believing what we're told about what products are worth instead of determining those products' value for ourselves, we're turning our version of capitalism into something else. We're withdrawing the consumer's power to shape the demand curve that is meant to keep the market at equilibrium. In the swordfight of supply and demand, we're laying down our weapons and bowing before the supply curve, letting producers take over and tell us what we want—and at what price.

To be a skeptical consumer—to look past the tastemakers and magazines, to experience the liquid and judge wine on its pure underlying merits, and to learn about the wine while you're at it—is to flex the fingers of capitalism's invisible hand, to push the system to work the way Adam Smith imagined that it could work. To surrender, instead, to the siren song of marketing and price signals—to buy what you're told to buy without questioning it, or to assume that expensive means good—is to withdraw your own brain from free participation in our own market economy. It is more than just self-destructive. It is, to me, un-American.

Chapter 6 The culture war

> No man also having drunk old wine
> straightway desireth new: for he saith,
> The old is better.
> –*King James Bible,* Luke 5:39

Let us turn, then, to what wine we like and don't like when we actually *do* hide the label. The wine industry is in a culture war. Expensive wine is getting more expensive, cheap wine is getting cheaper, French wine is in crisis, and consolidation has shaken the small-producer scene. To add to the chaos, as I've discussed above, the magazine critics' point ratings for wines on the 100-point scale—key determinants of market price and success—seem to be unrelated to everyday consumer preferences.

Although our blind tasters preferred cheaper wines to more expensive wines on the whole, what was equally dramatic was their degree of disagreement *with each other*. Some people liked wines with low sugar and high acidity, while others liked precisely the opposite: sweet, low-acidity wines. Why can't we all just get along?

There is, first and foremost, a genetic component to taste. Linda Bartoshuk, a professor at Yale Medical School, has famously divided people into three groups, which she calls "super-tasters," "tasters," and "non-tasters." Super-tasters, which are said to encompass about 25% of the population, have a higher than normal sensitivity to certain tastes; "tasters" (50% of the population) have a normal sensitivity; and "non-tasters" (the remaining 25%) have a lower sensitivity.[23]

Dyeing a portion of your tongue blue and counting the number of fungiform papillae within a certain radius can indicate which category you fall into, as can (under certain controlled circumstances) a taste of litmus paper that's been soaked with a chemical known as 6-n-propylthiouracil (PROP). The PROP litmus paper tastes unbearably bitter to super-tasters, bitter to tasters, and like ordinary paper to non-tasters, although bitterness ratings then have to be benchmarked for intensity bias.

In general (though by no means in every case), super-tasters tend to be picky eaters; they tend to find the spice of chili pepper and the bitterness in black coffee, spinach, and Brussels sprouts to be unpleasantly intense. Non-tasters, on the other hand, tend to like most things, and even (in survey results) tend to choose restaurants based more on atmosphere than on food. There has been little work done on the correlations between wine preferences and super-taster status, and it could turn out to be a fruitful (fruity?) area of research.

What is even more important in the perception of food and wine, though, is your sense of smell, and although there hasn't been a Bartoshuk-like breakthrough dividing people into olfactory groups, some people do have stronger senses of smell than others. In particular, it is well established that women have more acute senses of smell than men, while both genders are known to have diminished senses of smell as they age. But I'd love to see more research done on human differences in olfactory sensitivity.

Your upbringing can also impact your likes and dislikes in wine. Just as your taste and smell experience can change at a moment's notice when you think you're drinking an expensive wine, your experience can change over time as you acquire preferences for new or different tastes and smells; in psychology and neuroscience, this phenomenon is known as perceptual learning. Most of us have experienced some version of it as we've grown up. Maybe you didn't like mushrooms or blue cheese when you were a little kid, for instance—and maybe you didn't like wine at all the first time you tried it.

One thing that kids almost universally like is sugar, and our culture has become uniquely indulgent of that taste. People make a big deal about how American children are growing up on fast food, but at least fast food, for the most part, tastes good. However unhealthy a McDonald's Quarter Pounder with Cheese is, and however suspect the provenance of its ingredients, the burger is well seasoned and has a reasonable balance of tastes and textures. What's totally out of balance, though, is the flavor profile of soft drinks. The silent killer of our nation's palate is sugar. Children are building up such a tolerance for sweet things at an early age—and in terms of gustatory tolerance, artificial sweeteners are just as bad as sugar—that sweetness has started to dominate the taste of foods whose traditional recipes don't even call for sugar, such as salad dressing. As a result, when many Americans start drinking wine, they don't even perceive wines like Yellow Tail to be sweet.

But genetics and upbringing don't tell the whole story of our differences in wine preference. Perceptual learning doesn't stop in adulthood, and when people study wine, formally or informally, their preferences change, too. When our statistical team looked more closely at our blind tasting data, we noticed a highly significant difference between the preferences of wine experts and everyday wine drinkers. While everyday wine drinkers preferred cheaper wines to expensive wines even more strongly than the group at large ($p=0.012$), wine experts—defined as people who have wine training, such as a sommelier course, or professional industry experience, tend to assign ratings as high, or even higher, for expensive wines than they do for cheaper wines.

And when we zoomed in on the results—cutting off the top and bottom 10% of the price range—that difference became even more pronounced. (See Appendix 2 for details.) This indicates to me that wine professionals, through their experience, are acquiring a taste for a different style of wine—a more expensive style.

What kind of perceptual learning is going on when people become wine experts? What is it, exactly, that makes more expensive wine better in the eyes of professionals?

That is the question at the heart of the culture war, and the reason it's a war is that many professionals don't even agree with each other. People's preferences in wine vary wildly, even within the ranks of those that have gone through extensive training. In my view, one reason for this divide is that wine has never had a single style or a single purpose. Is it meant to be served before dinner, with dinner, or with dessert? Is it meant to be drunk in your living room, on the beach, or at a world-class restaurant? The answer to all of these questions is yes, and the answers to what wine should taste like are different in each case.

When you figure in genetic differences, differences in upbringing, differences in understanding about what purpose wine is supposed to serve, and differences in mood or body chemistry on a given day or at a given moment, blind tasting data become so noisy that you need to collect thousands of data points, as we did, to get any statistically significant results at all. This is true even when the tasters are all experienced wine professionals. "Variation in judgment, even among experts," write Amerine and Roessler, "is why we reject single-judge evaluations."

Yet the world of wine criticism is coming to be dominated by exactly those types of single-judge evaluations. The culture war is being won, through brute force, by individuals like Robert Parker and the *Wine Spectator* critics, who have come together to promote a unified, but narrow, vision of what "quality" means in wine. As the schools that train sommeliers and wine professionals have come aboard, too, a newly formed consensus about quality has begun to re-shape the world's basic definition of what wine is supposed to taste like. Through perceptual learning, an entire generation of wine experts is being trained to believe that the style of wine that Robert Parker likes is worth paying extra money for.

The single most recognizable aspect of the style that Parker likes is that it plays to America's sweet tooth. The style is specific, it's easily identifiable, and it is more commonly found in wines made by modern producers from the New World (e.g. the United States and Australia) than wines made by traditional producers from the Old World (e.g. France, Spain, Portugal, and Italy).[24] Parker's influence is so powerful that many Old World wineries are converting to the New World style.

Proponents of the New World style tend to describe it with words like jammy, fruit-forward, big, full-bodied, and concentrated. Opponents of the style tend to call it aggressive, in-your-face, overextracted, overly alcoholic, unbalanced, and sometimes even sweet. Opponents also complain that New World methods create similar wines, regardless of the region, resulting in a convergence of the world's wine styles and a loss of diversity.

In its more expensive incarnations, the New World style often has noticeable flavors of wood, toast, and vanilla, which come from oak-barrel aging, or, in more inexpensive wines, from the addition of oak chips to the vat. The proponents of the New World style tend to like that noticeably oaky flavor, and the opponents don't, complaining that it throws the wine out of balance.

As for the Old World style, its proponents like to talk about it as balanced, elegant, sometimes austere, and, at its best, faithfully representatitve of a particular terroir (the unique characteristics of a region's geography, climate, soil, and so on); opponents tend to describe it as harsh, acidic, bitter, thin, or astringent. You're more likely to find tannins in cheap Old World wines than in cheap New World wines, although more expensive New World wines often have them, too.

Both proponents and opponents of the Old World style seem to agree that Old World wine, because of its more subtle qualities, often takes more time to mature than does New World wine; the proponents tend to see this as a virtue that rewards patience, while the opponents see it as an outdated inconvenience (although they might just call themselves "realists," given how hard it is these days to find a restaurant or wine store that sells older vintages).

Fueled by the magazine critics, who often seem to reserve their highest ratings for big, concentrated wines, the New World style is poised to wipe the Old World style off the map in the realms of both expensive and cheap wine. The runaway success of the Australian wine brand Yellow Tail—whose Chardonnay and Shiraz are now the world's two best-selling bottles, each selling more than 20 million bottles per year—has put a nail into the coffin of a French inexpensive-to-midpriced-wine industry that was already reeling from a weak dollar and softening domestic demand.

Yellow Tail Shiraz is like a caricatured example of the New World style, so dominated by oak, alcohol, and concentrated fruit flavors that it barely tastes like wine—or, at least, it barely tastes like wine *used* to taste. Wine industry consultant Jon Fredrikson, in an interview with the *New York Times*, has called Yellow Tail "the perfect wine for a public grown up on soft drinks."[25]

Perhaps, then, it shouldn't be surprising that Robert Parker has called the Yellow Tail wines "surprisingly well-made": he, too, grew up on soft drinks. According to Elin McCoy, his biographer, Parker hadn't had a single glass of dry wine until he was twenty years old, on his first trip to France: "Since Coca-Cola was so expensive, a dollar for a tiny bottle, Pat [his girlfriend] insisted he try *un verre du vin*, the first dry wine Parker had ever tasted."[26]

Whether or not you find the "Parkerized" style pleasant on a sensory level, a more fundamental problem is that it's a style of wine that's not created by nature, but rather by aggressive intervention with techniques like aging wine in new oak barrels for extended periods of time. What's even more bothersome, though, is the fact that, driven by the ratings of Parker and his progeny, the worlds of cheap and expensive wines all over the world seem to be converging on a single taste profile. As "Parkerization" is being introduced to Old World regions such as Spain, France, and Italy, the traditional style that has produced unique local wines in those regions is being replaced with one common "international" style that's geared toward getting high scores from magazine critics like Parker and *Wine Spectator*.

Even within France, Parker is famous for preferring Bordeaux to Burgundy, and his power is such that many top Burgundian wines are currently marginalized in the marketplace when compared with top Bordeaux wines. As a result, even in Burgundy there is now a push to make wines in a more concentrated, oaky style, which is totally antithetical to the region's historical character.

As the world's wines grow more similar to each other with each successive vintage, the incredible diversity of the world's wine regions is being lost, and—perhaps due to undue deference to the magazine critics' ratings—the world's high-end wine consumers are supporting the trend with their wallets.

Whatever style of wine you *think* you like, you owe it to yourself, and to the wine world, to test that assumption scientifically. If you're a wine beginner, you might start with the suggested contrast tests I've set up in chapter 8. Either way, it's important make sure you *agree* with the magazine critics, at least, before jumping onto the New World bandwagon.

Maybe for *you*, a bottle of Dom Pérignon, Screaming Eagle, or Château Pétrus really *is* worth the $150, $2,000, or $5,000 that it's commanding. Either way, once you've decided for yourself—

firsthand and blind, with only your palate in charge—whether or not the Emperor is dressed in each of these categories, your brain's curious habit of making things taste like you expect them to taste—of making expensive things taste better, and of making cheap things taste worse—might lessen, too.

That's the funny thing about our brains, and about expectations. If this book makes you skeptical of high price tags, just reading it could change the taste of expensive wine for you. What will change your experience even more, though, is blind tasting yourself. By questioning wine prices, you will become less of a slave to expectations and more of a student of your own palate. Invoking only the simple, everyday miracle of the scientific method, you will have turned a placebo into wine.

Chapter 7 Our wine trials

Our wine trials were held between April 2007 and February 2008. During that time, Alexis and I held a total of 17 brown-bag blind tastings at restaurants, bars, and at private residences in states of New York, Massachusetts, Connecticut, and Texas. 507 tasters participated, tasting and rating 560 different wines.

Alexis and I designed the wine rating forms for the trials in conjunction with two winemakers, Julian Faulkner and Isaure de Pontbriand; Jay Emerson, who is on the statistics faculty at Yale; and Jake Katz, the Fearless Critic statistician. Jay and Jake are the co-authors of appendix 1, which explains the design of the experiment and the structure of our blind tastings in more technical detail.

Julian and Isaure had served as judges in various wine juries and medal competitions for publications such as France's preeminent *Guide Hachette*, and Julian had plenty of criticisms of the way these tastings had generally been conducted: fluffy methodology, too few judges, unscientific results.

We wanted to design rating forms that were user-friendly and straightforward enough for everyday wine drinkers; that allowed wine experts the flexibility to express themselves; and that could be completed within the time constraints of our blind tastings. We settled on six wines per flight, the number that we found could be evaluated in about 45 minutes without palate fatigue. Below is a replica of the form we used in our tastings.

Another issue that came up—an issue that hadn't been confronted in any of Julian's and Isaure's collective experience in wine juries—was how to deal with the difference between tasters that were paying close attention to the wines and tasters that weren't, and how to deal with the difference between tasters that had sensitive palates and tasters that didn't.

overall

How do you find the wine?

bad	okay	good	great
☐	☐	☐	☐

nose

How do you find the aromas?

bad	okay	good	great
☐	☐	☐	☐

How intense are the aromas?

faint	not very intense	intense	very intense
☐	☐	☐	☐

mouth

How do you find the taste?

bad	okay	good	great
☐	☐	☐	☐

How intense is the taste?

faint	not very intense	intense	very intense
☐	☐	☐	☐

How long is the finish?

very short	short	medium	long
☐	☐	☐	☐

notes

Notes on aromas, tastes, texture, and finish: (Use reverse side if you like.)

What do you like most about the wine? (Be sarcastic if you like.)

What do you like least about the wine? (Be brutally honest.)

More to
say?
Flip this
page and
write on
the reverse.

How much would you be willing to pay for a bottle in a store? $

Rather than weighing the opinions of all tasters equally or favoring the opinions of self-proclaimed wine experts, we wanted to insert an objective measurement of each taster's ability, degree of consistency, or trustworthiness, and then to weight his or her ratings according to that evaluation.

Our solution was the twin-wine test. The idea was to plant two identical wines within a flight of six (unbeknownst to the taster, of course), and then to compare the taster's rankings of the two. If a taster ranked two identical wines very far apart from each other, how could he or she be trusted to evaluate wines in general? Either he or she wasn't paying attention; he or she didn't have a palate sensitive enough to detect that the wines are similar; or he or she just wasn't very good at comparatively evaluating wines.

We chose Yellow Tail Shiraz, the world's bestselling single red wine, to use for the twin-wine test, and our statistics team adjusted weights accordingly. If someone tasted 6 wines against each other and ranked the two Yellow Tail Shiraz bottles #1 and #6, we valued his or her opinion very weakly. On the other hand, if he or she ranked the two Yellow Tails right next to each other (e.g. #2 and #3), we valued his or her opinion very strongly. Tasters who performed in between got in-between weightings.

To my knowledge, this was the first time a twin-wine test had been employed in a wine jury in order to variably weight tasters' ratings according to their degree of consistency—or, to put it more simply, I believe this to be the first wine guide to confront the problem that some wine tasters are more sensitive than others to the differences between wines.

To help you understand our project better, the pages that follow will take you on a visual tour of the tastings that were held in restaurants and bars.

Lotus, New York City

The venue for our inaugural blind tasting was the legendary velvet-rope nightclub and restaurant Lotus, in New York's meatpacking district. Lotus hosted more than 50 sommeliers, wine writers, winemakers, and everyday wine drinkers, all of whom braved the biggest thunderstorm of the year in New York City to join us as blind tasters.

Café Josie, Austin, Texas
The first Texas tasting was held in chef-owner Charles Mayes' intimate, inventive restaurant in Austin's Clarksville neighborhood. Café Josie's culinary concept brings together tropical flavors and Southwestern spices. The restaurant's wine director tasted with us, as did local wine bloggers, writers, and a rigorous group of Austin-area foodies, wine experts, and college professors.

Aquavit Restaurant, New York City

To celebrate the release of his cookbook, *The Soul of a New Cuisine: A Discovery of the Foods and Flavors of Africa*, celebrity chef Marcus Samuelsson cooked an African dinner at his flagship restaurant, Aquavit, for an illustrious cross-section of New York food and wine aficionados. Clare Murumba, with whom I co-authored the restaurant guide *The Menu: New Haven*, organized the dinner, which was preceded by a one-flight blind tasting for *The Wine Trials*.

Bella's, New York City

Bella's is a fashionable candlelit bar lined with books for an evocative library-lounge vibe. It's hidden beneath Bar Martignetti in Manhattan's NoLita. More than 75 blind tasters attended our most social tasting, including food and wine experts, New York City area Harvard alumni, Fodor's travel editors, and SNL writers.

Yale Club of Houston, Texas

Carol and Andy Vickery hosted the Yale Club of Houston's fall gathering, which brought in an assortment of Yale alumni of all ages, from all walks of life, each of whom blind-tasted one flight.

Seppi's, Parker Meridien Hotel, New York City

Claude Solliard's authentic French bistro in midtown Manhattan's Parker Meridien Hotel turns out flawless versions of classics like steak tartare and Alsatian tarte flambée. Seppi's hosted this relaxed midweek afternoon blind tasting, which included French chefs, sommeliers, oenologists, filmmakers, novelists, and students and alumni of the French Culinary Institute, my gustatory alma mater.

Haynes & Boone, Houston, Texas

A tasting in one of Houston's most scenic conference rooms, with sweeping views over the cityscape, was organized by Mark Trachtenberg and Abigail Roth and hosted by the Haynes & Boone law firm. It was a chance for Houston-area Yale Law alumni to catch up, blind-taste Champagnes and sparkling wines, and reminisce about what Bill and Hillary were like in law school.

Bistro Lancaster, Houston, Texas

Up-and-coming chef Jamie Zelko has re-energized the traditional American menu at one of the grand dames of downtown Houston hotels, but the atmosphere—dark walls, low ceilings, white linens—is still a throwback. In addition to a great Houston food and wine crowd, we had tasters and sommeliers come in from Austin for the event.

Le Petit Café, Branford, Connecticut

Chef-owner Roy Ip's unpretentious French bistro, located about 20 minutes east of New Haven along the shoreline, is probably the best restaurant in Connecticut. The restaurant's bustling Parisian vibe paired well with a tasting that brought in a well-rounded panel of tasters from the New Haven area that included chefs, physicians, economists, art historians, and food bloggers.

Upstairs on the Square, Cambridge, Massachusetts

This space was once occupied by Grendel's Den, a favorite college haunt that once competed with the Mask and Spear for Harvard Square customers. Upstairs on the Square has a more upmarket vibe, which worked well for the blind Champagne and sparkling wine tasting that we held for a small group of economists and Harvard and MIT faculty.

Del Raye, Northampton, Massachusetts

For the better part of a decade, Del Raye has been one of the best upmarket restaurants in my hometown of Northampton. Claudio Guerra and Bill Collins hosted two tastings here, which featured chefs and sommeliers from the Spoleto Group—including local restaurants Spoleto, Pizzería Paradiso, and Mama Iguana's—along with members of the local wine trade.

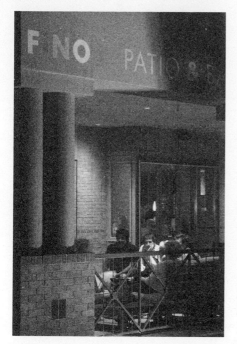

Fino Restaurant, Austin, Texas

The Spanish-inspired menu at this hip-but-mellow restaurant highlights underappreciated ingredients like white anchovies, mint, Medjool dates, and hanger steak—and underappreciated wines like dry sherry. A diverse crew of Austin-area chefs, sommeliers, and writers, along with wine experts from Fino's staff, joined us to blind taste just before the holidays.

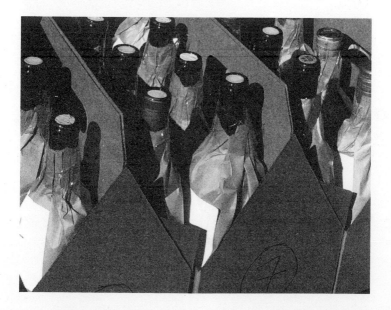

Chapter 8 Your wine trials

To blind taste yourself, you don't need to be as obsessive-compulsive about blind tasting as we were. At home, or even at a BYO restaurant, it's fairly easy to blind taste two to six wines at a time. Palate fatigue can set in for some people when you hit the seventh or eighth wine, and it's also difficult to rank wines against each other when more than six are involved. I recommend splitting wines into flights of six or fewer.

Our tasting forms can be downloaded in PDF format from www.thewinetrials.com. Brown lunch bags from the supermarket work well to conceal wines, and packing tape does a decent job of sealing them in. Champagne buckets, beach pails, large plastic tumblers, or cocktail shakers will all work as spit buckets; even if you don't plan to spit, you'll need buckets for dumping out remaining wine between tastes. Beyond that, the key ingredients are wine, patient friends, and lots of matching glasses. (Differently shaped glasses can have different effects on the wine, although this effect has been grossly exaggerated by glassware companies.)

The ideal glasses for blind tasting are seven-ounce (155 mL) ISO tasting glasses, designed by scientists in France to concentrate the aromas at exactly the point where your nose sticks into the glass. They're small enough to fit many on a table, and their tapered shape is also designed to allow for vigorous swirling without spillage. These are the glasses used in many wine industry conventions and fairs, and they are what we used in our blind tastings. We have posted information about where to order them on www.thewinetrials.com.

If you can't find ISO-certified tasting glasses, then be sure, at a minimum, that your glasses curve inward at the top and aren't merely cylindrical.

If you're doing an informal tasting at a party, there are really only three important rules to keep in mind: first, the person who bagged the wines shouldn't be the same person who numbers the bottles. (A Sharpie marker works well for bag-numbering, by the way.) Second, tasters shouldn't be allowed to discuss wines with each other before assigning their ratings—that will introduce serious bias toward the opinions of the more self-confident people in the group. Third, tasters shouldn't be allowed to change their ratings after the wines have been exposed. Of course, it goes without saying that tasters shouldn't be told *anything* about the wine they're tasting beforehand—not even the country of origin or grape, and certainly not the price range.

If you want to do a more formal tasting, however, there are several other things you should keep in mind. First, you should transfer screwcap wines into empty non-screwcap bottles to avoid bias, because the threads will be visible even after the wine is brown-bagged. Magnums, jug wines, and box wines should also be transferred to normal 750 mL bottles in the same way; if you blind taste much, it's a good idea to keep a few empty wine bottles around the house.

Unless you're tasting older vintages, wines should be left uncorked for a minimum of 45 minutes before serving to let them breathe and minimize reductive qualities that can taint wine aromas, particularly with screwcap wines. White wines should be tasted above the temperature at which you would normally drink them; it's easier to tell the difference between wines when they're warmer. Taste white wines around 55°F to 60°F (13°C to 16°C). In general, taking whites from the refrigerator, opening them, and leaving them to breathe at room temperature for the requisite 45 minutes should do the trick. Red wines should be tasted around 60°F to 65°F (16°C to 18°C).

With respect to pouring wines, there are two methods that work, depending on how many glasses you have. The method that best allows for wine-against-wine comparison is to distribute one glass for each wine to each taster, and to pour all the wines at once. So if you had four tasters and six wines, you'd need 24 glasses. (If you don't have a dishwasher, you'll hate this method.) Logistically speaking, this won't work with full-sized wine glasses if you're tasting more than two or three wines, because they'll take up too much room on the table; ISO-sized glasses will work, though.

The second method, which is more suitable for large numbers of people, is to give the tasters one glass each and let them pour wines themselves as they go. In that case, after tasting each wine, tasters should rinse their glasses with the next wine to be tasted before pouring the full tasting portion. When rinsing, tasters should make an effort to coat the whole inside surface of the glass with the new wine while holding the glass upside down over the spit bucket and slowly pouring it out. Once the glass is coated, tasters can then pour a full tasting portion of the next wine.

When the wines are served, every taster should be given a rating form and a pen. Serve plain water crackers (Carr's plain flavor is reliably neutral) at the table to cleanse the palate between wines. Some people like to drink water between wines as well, although it's not as good a palate cleanser as crackers.

Encourage tasters to pour two-ounce tasting portions, to take at most one swallow of each wine, and to spit on repeated tastes. (Very few people will get wasted on six swallows of wine, and some people—I'm on the fence—feel that something is lost on the finish if you don't swallow at least once.) If tasters are tempted to drink more than that, remind them that once the tasting is finished and the bottles are exposed, they can drink as much as they want.

Encourage your tasters to taste the wines in random order. It's well established in the field of psychology that tasters have a positive bias towards the first item tasted or rated in a series, and in our tastings we took steps to ensure that tasters did not all taste in the same order.

Tasters should both rate and rank the wines. Ranking is a more accurate way of scoring wines *against each other*, because it forces tasters to make tough decisions, but rating is the best way to compare wines from one flight or tasting to wines from another. Our rating scale is intentionally simple, and we have four rating check boxes—as opposed to five—so that tasters are forced to make the tough decision between the second and third, rather than falling back on an indecisive middle choice. Accordingly, you should not allow tasters to check between boxes.

When all the tasters are done rating, make it clear that people are no longer allowed to make changes to their forms, and then, with great fanfare and drama, expose the wines. Don't forget to immediately record which wine corresponds to which bag number. The simplest way of scoring the wines is called a "rank sum": you add up all the tasters' rankings, and the lowest score wins. To calculate a total *rating*, count one point for every bad vote, two for okay, three for good, four for great, and the highest score wins.

However many of these rules get thrown out, try to remember, above all else, that even a taster under the influence of alcohol is better than a taster under the influence of others—or of the label.

The following series of head-to-head blind taste tests is designed to help you understand the differences between the style categories that we've used for the reviews in this book—and, more generally, to help illuminate your own preferences in wine style. These are tests designed for people that have little experience with wine tasting—a way to start getting a basic sense of the axes on which wines differ. For each head-to-head blind tasting, I've suggested wines from our top 100 that are representative of each style, although similar wines can be substituted.

I suggest doing these blind tastings in simple pairs, on their own, although you can also combine two or three of the pairs into one larger flight; if you do so, though, stick to all whites or all reds. Equipped with the results of these comparisons, you'll be able to narrow down your choice of wine—not just within our top 100, but also, say, when you're in a wine store looking for something new and different from a small producer.

Keep in mind, however, that different styles of wine have their time and place. No matter how much you like light Old World white wines, you wouldn't want to drink one with a steak. Nor would you want to drink a heavy New World red on the beach, whatever your degree of fondness for California Cabernet.

New World vs. Old World: reds
Rosemount Shiraz (New World) vs.
Marqués de Cáceres Rioja Crianza (Old World)

New World vs. Old World: whites
3 Blind Moose Chardonnay (New World) vs.
Feudi di San Gregorio Falanghina (Old World)

Light vs. heavy: reds
Cavit Merlot (light) vs.
Concannon Petite Sirah (heavy)

Light vs. heavy: whites
Crane Lake Sauvignon Blanc (light) vs.
Fat Bastard Chardonnay (heavy)

Sweet vs. dry: rosé
Any White Zinfandel (sweet) vs.
Parallèle 45 Côtes du Rhone Rosé (dry)

Sweet vs. dry: reds
Mavrodaphne of Patras (sweet) vs.
Vin de Crete (dry)

Aromatic vs. crisp: whites
Château Ste. Michelle Riesling (aromatic) vs.
Huber Hugo Grüner Veltliner (crisp)

Pinot Noir vs. Cabernet Sauvignon: reds
Mark West Pinot Noir vs.
Liberty School Cabernet Sauvignon

Low acidity vs. high acidity: whites
Grand Pacific Starliner white (low acidity) vs.
Oyster Bay Sauvignon Blanc (high acidity)

Expensive vs. inexpensive: sparkling wines
Veuve Clicquot Ponsardin Champagne ($45) vs.
Domaine Ste. Michelle Brut ($12)

Chapter 9 The verdict

In the pages that follow, the authors and editors recommend and review 100 wines under $15 that beat $50 to $150 bottles in our blind tastings. Throughout this book, I've shown that people's tastes differ dramatically, and that even your own tastes are highly suggestible. If you've taken this book seriously so far, then you might take our selections with a grain of salt. But I hope that our results will serve, at least, as a useful starting point for your own blind tasting journey.

Since this book is intended to reach a large audience, we have limited our scope to the universe of mass-market wines that are commonly available around the country—at supermarkets, liquor stores, groceries, and specialty chains—not just at boutique wine stores. To assemble the initial group of more than 500 commonly available wines to taste, we began with the top-selling bottles under $15 from the so-called "control states"—US states where all alcohol sold must go through the government. The National Alcohol Beverage Control Association provided us with a record of every case of wine sold in those states in 2006.

We expanded that list by adding wines from the top 30 wine companies by annual revenues as reported in *Wine Business Monthly*, and the 100 top-selling wine brands as reported in *Restaurant Wine* newsletter. Finally, we visited branches of major retail chains such as Whole Foods, Trader Joe's, and Costco, and we added dozens of wines frequently found in one or more of those stores. For comparative purposes, we added a stratified random sample of more expensive bottles from both the New World and the Old World, but those bottles, of course, were not considered for our top 100.

There are many excellent values under $15 from smaller producers that unfortunately did not meet our criteria for widespread availability. That's why it's doubly important to use this book as a jumping-off point to create your own top 100. In a sophisticated wine store, the best place to start is often with the wines you *haven't* heard of—not because wines from obscure regions or producers are necessarily *better*, but because you're not paying a premium for a name-brand region or producer. A good wine store employee can be more helpful than a magazine critic. But nothing can substitute for taking the wine home and blind-tasting it yourself against other wines.

When the results were tabulated from the blind tastings, and the scores calculated by our statisticians, the editors re-tasted (blind, of course) the top-scoring inexpensive wines that had beat out the expensive wines. Of those, we chose 100 winning wines that held broad appeal to both groups in our tastings: the wine experts and the everyday wine drinkers. All 100 recommended wines were selected for inclusion before we knew what they were—before they'd been removed from their brown bags.

You'll notice that, unlike the rest of the book, the reviews are written in first-person plural ("we"); that's because they represent a joint effort between Alexis and me, the editors, and our blind tasters. In general, we tried to highlight sensory notes that were shared by multiple blind tasters, not just one taster's flight of fancy, although the latter was sometimes so amusing that we couldn't help ourselves. (Some good comments didn't make it in the book because the wine didn't qualify, like one taster's succinct description of Sutter Home White Zinfandel: "If Jesus tasted this wine, he'd turn it back to water.")

After the wines were revealed, we also added non-blind portions of review text discussing the producer, grapes, bottle design, and so on; but we did not change any tasting notes or descriptions, nor did we change any decisions about which wines would be included.

Although all 100 wines in this book are recommended—they represent the very top wines out of the 560 tasted—we have also offered special recognition to the #1 wines in each of the style categories. Wines are categorized along the following axes: red and white; New World and Old World (see chapter 6); and heavy and light. Heavy vs. light is a subjective distinction, to be sure, but one we hope you'll get used to; roughly speaking, it corresponds with alcohol content, thickness of texture, intensity of flavor, and what wine people call "body," but that doesn't fully capture the distinction. There are also special categories for rosé, sparkling wines, and sweet or aromatic wines, for a total of 11 categories.

Wines that won their style category are marked with a special logo on their page. We've also selected four wines that didn't win their categories but we thought deserved special recognition as an excellent wine or a notable value. Those are marked with the "Editors' pick" logo.

In our reviews, we've tried to use everyday language to describe the wines—words that will make sense to everyday wine drinkers as well as wine experts. We do use fruit flavors, of course; the English language doesn't really have any way of describing taste sensations without making reference to other taste sensations, the way it does for colors. But we've done our best to stick to familiar flavors. We'll talk about orange or grapefruit, not gooseberry or elderflower.

The only two wine buzzwords we use consistently are "tannins" and "acidity." Tannins are the quality (found only in red wines) that dry out the mouth; acidity is the opposite, the quality that makes your mouth water. We also review the design of each bottle—after all, as this book has shown, that's a big part of what you're buying. The average retail price in the book is found in a circle in the upper right-hand corner of the page. A white circle means a white wine, a red circle means a red wine, and a gray circle means a rosé. Sparkling wines have bubbles coming out of a white circle. Each review page also specifies the wine's region, vintage tasted, suggested food pairings (which are utterly subjective, of course), and grape varieties.

Speaking of grape varieties, you might be wondering why we don't categorize wines on that axis, as many wine guides do. There's a reason for this: although wines are indexed by grape variety in the book index, our view is that, especially for inexpensive wines, categorization by grape variety can often be misleading and unhelpful. Certainly, in some cases, varieties do influence the taste of the wine—especially extremely acidic grapes like Sauvignon Blanc, or sweet or aromatic grapes like Muscat or Gewürztraminer—but in inexpensive wines, this effect is often minimal compared with the Old World-New World divide or the light-heavy style divide. For example, a Merlot from Bordeaux would probably tend to taste more like a Cabernet Sauvignon from Bordeaux than like a Merlot from the United States.

You might notice a few interesting trends in our top 100: for example, for all the fanfare about good values coming from Australia, only 5 of the 60 wines we blind-tasted from Australia made the top 100. In general, tasters didn't like the Aussie wines' over-the-top sweetness and lack of balance. On the whole, rosés fared even worse, probably because so many of them were sweet; of 47 rosés tasted, 35 were sweet wines like White Zinfandel, of which not one made the top 100. Even the remaining 12, which were purportedly dry, often showed more sweetness than blind tasters would have liked. On the other hand, there were strong showings from France and the Iberian peninsula; these wines showed more balance than most, and many have been able to maintain strong value propositions even with the weak dollar.

On our website, www.thewinetrials.com, we plan to post information about virtual national wine tastings in which anyone in the world can participate, as well as limited-participation in-person tastings that we will continue to hold around the country.

In the meantime, I hope that you find our recommendations helpful. Think of them as a headstart on your own blind tasting journey. Even if you do not agree with all of our selections, I hope you'll use this book as a starting point to question your assumptions about wine pricing, to hold blind-tasting parties with your friends, and ultimately, to help restore the kind of order to the market that might only come from a grassroots movement of consumers that make a conscious decision to trust their own palates more than price tags.

Notes

1. You can read more about the Mask and Spear in an article in the centennial issue of *Harvard Magazine*, November 1998, by class of 1992 alumnus Adam Goodheart:
http://harvardmagazine.com/1998/11/freshman.html

2. Economists often use logarithmic price scales to analyze wine pricing, as we did; this helps to test the hypothesis that a wine's price might increase exponentially as its quality increases linearly.

3. Some people in the wine industry dispute the validity of tasting cheap wines against expensive wines, objecting that the former are generally easier to enjoy on their own, while the latter need to be served with food and/or need to age for several years. However, controlled wine tastings have long been the accepted industry standard for the evaluation of wines at any price range. It would seem implausible—and it would certainly introduce more sources of bias than it would mitigate—to conduct a wine tasting with food pairings. As for the question of age, older vintages of expensive wines are rarely available at most wine stores or restaurants, so they would not properly represent the wines people are actually buying and drinking. Tasting older wines would also increase the likelihood

of many other confounding factors, including improper storage, oxidation, and cork taint.

4. Robin Goldstein, Johan Almenberg, Anna Dreber, Alexis Herschkowitsch, and Jacob Katz, "Do More Expensive Wines Taste Better? Evidence from a Large Sample of US Blind Tastings," American Association of Wine Economists working paper #16, www.wine-economics.org/workingpapers. Also available at the Stockholm School of Economics website, http://swopec.hhs.se/hastef, and at www.thewinetrials.com.

5. Jancis Robinson, *Confessions of a Wine Lover* (Penguin Books, 1997).

6. Maynard Amerine and Edward Roessler, *Wines: Their Sensory Evaluation* (W.H. Freeman and Company, 1976).

7. Sébastien Lecocq and Michael Visser, "What Determines Wine Prices: Objective vs. Sensory Characteristics," *Journal of Wine Economics*, Vol. 1, No. 1 (May 2006).

8. When I refer to "Champagne," I mean only wines that come from the French Champagne appellation, which are rarely available for less than $25 and are often far more expensive than that.

9. Fréderic Brochet, "Chemical Object Representation in the Field of Consciousness" (application presented for the Grand Prix of the Académie Amorim following work carried out towards a doctorate from the Faculty of Oenology of Bordeaux, General Oenology Laboratory) 2001.

10. Ralph Allison and Kenneth Uhl, "Influence of Beer Brand Identification on Taste Perception," *Journal of Marketing Research*, Vol. 1, No. 3 (August 1964).

11. Leonard Lee, Shane Frederick, and Dan Ariely, "Try It, You'll Like It: The Influence of Expectation, Consumption, and Revelation on Preferences for Beer," *Psychological Science*, Vol. 17, No. 12 (December 2006).

12. Hilke Plassmann, John O'Doherty, Baba Shiv, and Antonio Rangel, "Marketing Actions Can Modulate Neural Representations of Experienced Pleasantness," *Proceedings of the National Academy of Sciences* (January 14, 2008), http://www.pnas.org/cgi/content/abstract/0706929105v1.

13. Statistics were taken from custom searches for wines $10 and under from the 2000 to 2007 vintages performed on both www.winespectator.com (subscribers only) and www.wineenthusiast.com (open to the public). 1,953 wines returned by the *Wine Enthusiast* search with prices listed as $0 were ignored.

14. Roman Weil, "Analysis of Reserve and Regular Bottlings: Why Pay for a Difference Only the Critics Claim to Notice?" *Chance*, Vol. 18, No. 3 (Summer 2005).

15. James Laube, Laube Unfined Blog, "When Tasting, Blind Offers Vision," www.winespectator.com/Wine/Blogs/Blog_Detail/0,4211,1426,00.html (October 4, 2007).

16. The website is not clear on how specific the regions or appellations with which *Wine Spectator* critics are provided prior to tasting, so I don't know if they're told wine is from its specific appellation, "Hermitage," or the more general region "Northern Rhône." However, Hermitage is listed on Spectator's wine review search page as one of the "Wine Regions," so it seems reasonable to assume that it fits into their definition of "region."

17. LVMH 2007 Annual Report, online at http://www.lvmh.com/comfi/pdf_gbr/LVMH2007AnnualReport.pdf.

18. Constellation 2007 Annual Report, online at http://library.corporate-ir.net/library/85/851/85116/items/252600/STZ_2007AR.pdf.

19. Justin Weinberg, "Taste How Expensive This Is," in *Wine & Philosophy: A Symposium on Thinking and Drinking*, ed. Fritz Allhoff (Blackwell Publishing, 2008).

20. "Hitting the spot," *The Economist*, January 17, 2008.

21. Eric Asimov, The Pour, "If I Only Knew When I Tasted It…" http://thepour.blogs.nytimes.com/2007/09/13/if-i-only-knew-when-i-tasted-it/ (September 13, 2007).

22. Eric Asimov, The Pour, "Judging the Judging," http://thepour.blogs.nytimes.com/2007/09/17/judging-the-judging/ (September 17, 2007).

23. Linda Bartoshuk, "Sweetness: History, Preference, and Genetic Variability," *Food Technology*, Vol. 45, No. 11 (November, 1991).

24. The "New World" designation also traditionally includes wines from Chile, Argentina, New Zealand, and South Africa, and the "Old World" designation generally includes all of Europe.

25. Frank J. Prial, "The Wallaby That Roared Across the Wine Industry," *New York Times* (April 23, 2006).

26. Elin McCoy, *The Emperor of Wine: The Rise of Robert M. Parker, Jr., and the Reign of American Taste* (Ecco, 2005).

100 recommended wines under $15
that beat $50 to $150 wines in our blind tastings

Category winners	Country	Price
Alice White Chardonnay (light white)	Australia	$7
Avalon Cabernet Sauvignon (heavy red)	United States	$14
Domaine Ste. Michelle Brut (sparkling)	US Northwest	$12
Feudi di San Gregorio Falanghina (light white)	Italy	$14
LAN Rioja Crianza (light red)	Spain	$12
Mark West Pinot Noir (light red)	United States	$11
Marqués de Cáceres Rioja (heavy white)	Spain	$10
Osborne Solaz (heavy red)	Spain	$9
Parallèle 45 Côtes du Rhône (rosé)	France	$12
Parducci Sustainable White (light white)	United States	$11
Samos Muscat (sweet white)	Greece	$10

Editors' picks	Country	Price
Aveleda Vinho Verde (light white)	Portugal	$6
Campo Viejo Rioja Crianza (light red)	Spain	$9
Freixenet Brut (sparkling)	Spain	$9
House Wine (heavy red)	US Northwest	$12

Light Old World white *21 wines under $15 tasted* | | Price
1	Feudi di San Gregorio Falanghina *winner*	Italy	$14
2	Aveleda Vinho Verde *editors' pick*	Portugal	$6
3	Huber Hugo Grüner Veltliner	Austria	$12
4	Kettmeir Pinot Grigio	Italy	$14
5	Lois Grüner Veltliner	Austria	$12
6	Casal Garcia Vinho Verde	Portugal	$8
7	Kiwi Cuvée (Underdog Wine Merchants)	France	$8
8	Santi Pinot Grigio	Italy	$13
9	Citra Pinot Grigio	Italy	$7
10	Fâmega Vinho Verde	Portugal	$7

Heavy Old World white *15 wines under $15 tasted* | | Price
1	Marqués de Cáceres Rioja *winner*	Spain	$10
2	Cave de Lugny Mâcon-Villages	France	$11
3	Parallèle 45 Côtes du Rhône Blanc	France	$12
4	Fat Bastard Chardonnay	France	$11

Light New World white *50 wines under $15 tasted* | | Price
1	Parducci Sustainable White *winner*	United States	$11
2	Oyster Bay Sauvignon Blanc	New Zealand	$13
3	Bogle Sauvignon Blanc	United States	$9
4	Cousiño Macul Riesling	Chile	$9
5	Sincerely Sauvignon Blanc	South Africa	$14
6	Harlow Ridge Pinot Grigio	United States	$10
7	Gato Negro Sauvignon Blanc	Chile	$6
8	Nobilo Sauvignon Blanc	New Zealand	$14
9	Château Ste. Michelle Sauvignon Blanc	US Northwest	$10
10	35° South Sauvignon Blanc	Chile	$9
11	Crane Lake Sauvignon Blanc	United States	$5
12	Château Ste. Michelle Pinot Gris	US Northwest	$13
13	Porcupine Ridge Sauvignon Blanc	South Africa	$13
14	Geyser Peak Sauvignon Blanc	United States	$10
15	Villa Maria Sauvignon Blanc	New Zealand	$13

Heavy New World white *89 wines under $15 tasted* | | Price
1	Alice White Chardonnay *winner*	Australia	$7
2	Morro Bay Chardonnay	United States	$10
3	Three Blind Moose Chardonnay	United States	$11
4	Trackers Crossing Chardonnay 365	Australia	$7
NR	Almaden Chardonnay	United States	$3
NR	Charles Shaw Chardonnay	United States	$3

Light Old World red *39 wines under $15 tasted*   *Price*

1	LAN Rioja Crianza *winner*	Spain	$12
2	Campo Viejo Rioja Crianza *editors' pick*	Spain	$9
3	Marqués de Cáceres Rioja Crianza	Spain	$14
4	Louis Latour Le Pinot Noir	France	$14
5	Cavit Merlot	Italy	$9
6	Santa Cristina (Antinori)	Italy	$10
7	Georges Duboeuf Beaujolais-Villages	France	$10
8	René Barbier Mediterranean Red	Spain	$6
9	Vin de Crete (Kourtaki)	Greece	$9
10	Pirovano Montepulciano d'Abruzzo	Italy	$8
11	Malenchini Chianti	Italy	$10
12	Mouton Cadet	France	$9

Heavy Old World red *18 wines under $15 tasted*   *Price*

1	Osborne Solaz *winner*	Spain	$9
2	Guigal Côtes du Rhône	France	$10
3	La Vieille Ferme Rouge	France	$8
4	Vitiano (Falesco)	Italy	$9
5	Perrin Côtes du Rhône Réserve	France	$10
6	Château La Grange Clinet	France	$14
7	Petit Bistro Cabernet Sauvignon	France	$9

Light New World red *52 wines under $15 tasted*   *Price*

1	Mark West Pinot Noir *winner*	United States	$11
2	Parducci Sustainable Red	United States	$11
3	Castillo de Molina Pinot Noir	Chile	$12
4	Cono Sur Pinot Noir	Chile	$10
5	Fetzer Valley Oaks Merlot	United States	$9
6	Robert Mondavi Pinot Noir	United States	$10
7	Nathanson Creek Merlot	United States	$6
NR	Carlo Rossi Paisano	United States	$2

Heavy New World red *135 wines under $15 tasted*   *Price*

1	Avalon Cabernet Sauvignon *winner*	United States	$14
2	Concannon Petite Sirah	United States	$14
3	House Wine *editors' pick*	US Northwest	$12
4	Terrazas de los Andes Malbec	Argentina	$10
5	Liberty School Cabernet Sauvignon	United States	$14
6	Morro Bay Cabernet Sauvignon	United States	$10
7	The Wolftrap (Boekenhoutskloof)	South Africa	$14
8	Full Circle Zinfandel	United States	$9
9	Barefoot Cabernet Sauvignon	United States	$6

Heavy New World red *continued*	Country	Price
10 Trapiche Malbec	Argentina	$10
11 Cono Sur Cabernet Sauvignon	Chile	$10
12 Columbia Crest Cabernet Sauvignon	US Northwest	$8
13 Barefoot Merlot	United States	$6
14 Black Box Cabernet Sauvignon	United States	$5
15 Vida Orgánica Malbec	Argentina	$9
16 Redwood Creek Cabernet Sauvignon	United States	$8
17 Casa Rey Malbec	Argentina	$9
18 Red Truck Petite Sirah	United States	$11
19 Alamos Malbec	Argentina	$10
20 Bogle Old Vine Zinfandel	United States	$11
21 Beringer Founders' Estate Cab. Sauv.	United States	$9
22 Rosemount Shiraz	Australia	$10
NR Charles Shaw Cabernet Sauvignon	United States	$3

Rosé *29 wines under $15 tasted*	Country	Price
1 Parallèle 45 Côtes du Rhône *winner*	France	$12
2 Marqués de Riscal Rioja	Spain	$10
3 Jindalee Estate	Australia	$7

Sweet or aromatic *51 wines under $15 tasted*		Price
1 Samos Muscat (white) *winner*	Greece	$10
2 Château Ste. Michelle Riesling (white)	US Northwest	$10
3 Mavrodaphne of Patras (red)	Greece	$9
4 Grand Pacific Starliner (white)	United States	$12

Sparkling *22 wines under $15 tasted*	Country	Price
1 Domaine Ste. Michelle Brut *winner*	US Northwest	$12
2 Freixenet Brut *editors' pick*	Spain	$9
3 Rotari Brut	Italy	$13
4 Lorikeet Brut	Australia	$9
5 Segura Viudas Brut Reserva	Spain	$8
6 Presto Prosecco Brut	Italy	$10
7 Zardetto Prosecco	Italy	$11
8 Freixenet Cordon Negro Extra Dry	Spain	$9

NR indicates an unranked bargain-basement selection.

Wine reviews

Alamos Malbec
Bodega Catena Zapata

Rank #19 of 135 heavy New World reds under $15 tasted
Country Argentina **Vintage tasted** 2006
Grapes Malbec
Drink with steak with creamed spinach
Website www.catenawines.com

This is the entry-level wine of the Argentine export industry's 800-pound gorilla. Catena's wines are much loved by the cheap wine cognoscenti. That said, among inexpensive Malbecs, our blind tasters preferred the more balanced Trapiche and Terrazas to the more New World-ish Alamos. But all three are big, great-value wines to drink with an enormous hunk of meat.

Nose The aromas—assertive, aggressive, and fruity—were deemed a little too strong by some blind tasters; some also noticed a slight vegetality.

Mouth It almost tastes sweet, with bold fruit flavors that border on the annoying—clearly, they know they're making this wine for the US market. The finish is lengthy.

Design A dark, heavy, tapered bottle, minimalist writing, and a symphonic Andes-scape create a rather imposing look, even if the contents are quite approachable.

Alice White Chardonnay

Rank #1 of 89 heavy New World whites under $15 tasted
Country Australia **Vintage tasted** 2006
Grapes Chardonnay
Drink with shellfish, risotto, white pasta dishes
Website www.alicewhite.com

We love to hate Australia's irritatingly popular "critter wine" producers, who often seem to spend more time drawing animal cartoons than making decent wine. Alice White's sprightly Chardonnay, however, is a happy exception to this rule, with an unusual balance that led our blind tasters to believe the wine was far more expensive than it really is.

Nose It's Australian, so the big, toasty flavors aren't surprising—though a hint of minerality is.

Mouth Oak becomes obvious on the mouth, especially as the wine opens up with time. Bright flavors of tropical fruit and an unusual dose of acidity (for a cheap Australian wine, anyway) hold it together.

Design The marketing team plays off just about every Aussie stereotype on the label, with the kangaroo roasting in the spirally sun. But the pleasantly austere sans-serif small-caps font beneath—not to mention the great taste—makes up for the clichés.

Almaden Chardonnay

$3

Rank Unranked bargain-basement selection
Country United States **Vintage tasted** Non-vintage
Grapes Chardonnay
Drink with salmon, Brussels sprouts, cold pasta salads
Website www.almaden.com

There was a strong consensus among our blind tasters that this wine was made for outdoor quaffing on a warm day. It's also suited to making white sangría or pouring a mid-afternoon drink—if you hide the bottle (or box) beneath the table. You'd be better off taking a liter of Pepsi to a dinner party than this, though—at least in terms of how impressed the party host will be. Instead, keep a six-dollar magnum at home.

Nose The aroma is bright with citrus and fruit, but it's all a little chemical-smelling.

Mouth It's an eminently sippable, light-bodied wine whose fruit fades away pretty quickly on the finish.

Design Box or bottle: it's up to you. Either way, it's hard not to look cheap when you have that hideous cursive letter A followed by caps. The magnum throws in tacky, trying-to-be-voluptuous swirled glass for added effect.

Avalon Cabernet Sauvignon
Napa Valley

Rank #1 of 135 heavy New World reds under $15 tasted
Country United States **Vintage tasted** 2005
Grapes Cabernet Sauvignon
Drink with broiled or grilled ribeye steak, chicken mole
Website www.avalonwinery.com

Aesthetically and taste-wise, this could pass for a $100 bottle. Avalon embodies everything you look for in an expensive Napa Cab. It bursts out of the gate with balanced power in the first sip. And if you're like us, you'll find that the effect only grows on you as you continue drinking it; the wine fills the mouth with dark, elegant richness, neither sweet nor overbearing—just completely faithful to its Napa roots.

Nose Aromas of chocolate and dark fruit are there, but they're the least expressive thing about this wine.

Mouth The attack is a bit sweet, but it's tempered by bitter chocolate, acidity, and tannins; several blind tasters noticed licorice, too.

Design This might be the best-looking bottle in this book. It's well textured, simple, powerful, and graceful—just like the wine. The warm color scheme is soothing, too. Bravo.

Aveleda Vinho Verde

Rank #2 of 21 light Old World whites under $15 tasted
Country Portugal **Vintage tasted** Non-vintage
Grapes Alvarinho, Loureiro, Trajadura
Drink with sushi, cold salads, gazpacho
Website www.aveleda.pt

At six bucks, this wine is one of the great steals of the book. Sometimes you'll even see it for $5 (though probably not for long, given the weakness of the dollar). It's lightly sparkling, in the classic Vinho Verde style. The word "verde" refers to the youthful greenness of the wine, which is what makes it great for cheap outdoor refreshment. Our skeleton in the closet: on a hot summer day, we drink it over ice.

Nose Citrus flavors—melon, lemon, apple, pear—dominate with a hint of spiciness beneath.

Mouth A remarkable number of our blind tasters noticed black pepper or burnt chilies. Some bottles have been sweeter than others, but the acidity's always reliably high, and that's really the point.

Design It's busy but harmonious, with an appropriately green bottle and a nostalgic and colorful label. Other versions of this bottle circulate, including a more attractive sepia-toned version.

Barefoot Cabernet Sauvignon

Rank #9 of 135 heavy New World reds under $15 tasted
Country United States **Vintage tasted** Non-vintage
Grapes Cabernet Sauvignon
Drink with Tex-Mex, barbecue, chili
Website www.barefootwine.com

Proof that being under the omnipotent Gallo umbrella doesn't necessarily entail an overextracted fate, this wine, frequently found at Trader Joe's, pleasantly surprised us all. It's the ultimate wine for grillling outdoors on a chilly day, with its deep, almost meaty flavors.

Nose This wine reminded a lot of us of being outside; our blind tasters smelled campfire, wood, and dirt.

Mouth The tasting note on the bottle brags that it's "jammy." If you're a jam hater, don't let this scare you; our blind tasters found chocolate and spicy black pepper, too. The wine's weakest point is a somewhat chemical finish.

Design A shiny metallic sticker, front and center, boasts of some second-rate wine award. Are we supposed to be impressed when just about every Barefoot wine gets one? Beneath, there's that bare foot, rendered only slightly less gross by watercolor.

Barefoot Merlot

$6

Rank #13 of 135 heavy New World reds under $15 tasted
Country United States **Vintage tasted** Non-vintage
Grapes Merlot
Drink with vegetable stews, roast turkey
Website www.barefootwine.com

We have been happily surprised by several of the Barefoot wines, especially given their bargain-bin prices and ready availability. They're made in mass quantities, but the wines still retain a lot of character, and in general, our blind tasters liked the Barefoot reds more than whites. Here, for instance we have a bold, spicy, versatile Merlot that's big enough to push it into the "heavy" category; it matches well with a variety of foods and situations.

Nose Spices were the most noted aroma, although some blind tasters identified a slightly off-putting chemical smell.

Mouth Dark tastes—chocolate, nuts, black fruit—lead into a great, long-lasting finish.

Design The gold medal seems slightly different on each bottle—but it always manages to seem plenty tacky, starburst and all. We do prefer the foot in blue, however, as it is on this bottle.

Beringer Cabernet Sauvignon

Founders' Estate

$9

Rank #21 of 135 heavy New World reds under $15 tasted
Country United States **Vintage tasted** 2004
Grapes Cabernet Sauvignon
Drink with roast beef, game birds, lentil soup
Website www.beringer.com

The folks at Beringer have really outdone themselves here...literally. This $9 wine outscored their own Beringer Private Reserve Cabernet Sauvignon—whose asking price is about $120. A "Goldilocks wine," as one blind taster called it, the Founders' Estate is middle-of-the-road enough to please everyone: not too sweet, not too tannic. So hold on to your Benjamins, and pay for this wine with a Thomas. After all, Jefferson was a wine buff—Franklin was more of a beer guy.

Nose The aroma is full of fruits that don't overwhelm the other elements of the wine once it's in your mouth.

Mouth Subtle hints of black pepper, as well as some red fruit, made our blind tasters happy.

Design Misguided. The strange swoop of the right side of the label just ends up looking like a mistake. But for a $111 savings, we can handle an ugly bottle.

Black Box Cabernet Sauvignon

$5

Rank #14 of 135 heavy New World reds under $15 tasted
Country United States **Vintage tasted** 2005
Grapes Cabernet Sauvignon
Drink with recently delivered pizza, mozzarella sticks
Website www.blackboxwines.com

If you've got any I'm-above-box-wine snobbery left in you, this wine will exorcise it. It's hard to call a box wine "upmarket," but at $20 for three liters, it almost sounds steep—until you do the math; that's the equivalent of four bottles. (For blind tasting purposes, we transferred this classic, if aroma-challenged, Cab to a regular bottle.) One of our blind tasters wrote that she would buy it as a gift for her parents; we wonder if her premise would hold once she saw the packaging. One major advantage of a box wine is that it keeps for days and days.

Nose You've got to inhale hard to get much on the nose here, and even then, it's just a bit of red fruit. The aromas aren't the strong point of the Black Box.

Mouth Some tasters were actually reminded of white wine, but almost all thought it was simple and easy to drink.

Design We applaud the container in general, but the label looks pulled from a bottle. Surely they could have had more fun with this format.

Bogle Old Vine Zinfandel

Rank #20 of 135 heavy New World reds under $15 tasted
Country United States **Vintage tasted** 2005
Grapes Zinfandel
Drink with roast lamb, merguez sausage, chocolate cake
Website www.boglewinery.com

Zinfandel was a divisive grape for our blind tasters—experts as well as everyday wine drinkers. The Zins that made the top 100 won't please everybody; they're concentrated, in-your-face, and to some people, just too sweet. But if Zinfandel is your thing, the Bogle is a totally honest version. It's a classic New World expression of the grape, with woodsy flavors, highly concentrated fruit, high alcohol (14.5%), and plenty of oak.

Nose Blind tasters identified sour cherry and medicinal notes—some people called it eucalyptus—with brambly, piney qualities.

Mouth Tasters found more of those brambly pine-forest notes, as well as hints of vanilla that come from oak.

Design This subtly tapered Bogle bottle is a model of power and elegance. The creeping, almost primordial vine graphic and deep black background seem to echo the wine's qualities.

Bogle Sauvignon Blanc

Rank #3 of 50 light New World whites under $15 tasted
Country United States **Vintage tasted** 2005
Grapes Sauvignon Blanc
Drink with pesto, cream of potato soup, Greek salad
Website www.boglewinery.com

A family-owned operation in Clarksburg, California, 40-year-old Bogle seems to have handled growth better than have most big-time producers. Take, for instance, this balanced, well crafted version of an American Sauvignon Blanc: it's subtle but expressive, and, most importantly, it's fun to drink. The acidity isn't overwhelming like it often is in New Zealand Sauvignon Blancs, but it's nicely capable of cutting through creamy dishes.

Nose A fairly faint aroma manages to waft green-citrusy fruit in a way that our blind tasters appreciated.

Mouth Some tasters found the wine a bit watery, but the flavors are bright, with lemon, flowers, and crisp acidity.

Design The effect of the Bogle taper is lessened by the wine's extremely pale color, which shows through the clear bottle. No design awards here, but it's inoffensive.

Campo Viejo Rioja Crianza

$9

Rank #2 of 39 light Old World reds under $15 tasted
Country Spain **Vintage tasted** 2006
Grapes Tempranillo, Garnacha, Mazuelo
Drink with roast duck, lamb, savory cheeses
Website www.campoviejo-usa.com

This wine reminds us what wine used to taste like before the emergence of the in-your-face "international" style. This one, though, is still old-school Old World, in that earthy, almost dirty way (in the very best sense of the word) that transports you to a more rustic place. Rioja Crianza is aged longer than most inexpensive wines, so it's mature, too—and complex. Some argue that Rioja needs to be drunk with food, but we'd drink this one anytime, any place. It's light enough not to overwhelm you as an apéritif, which is rare for an inexpensive red wine.

Nose This isn't the best the wine has to offer; expect some muted fruit and a slight chemical note.

Mouth An ever-so-slight viscosity and a long, beautiful finish round out the body. Tempranillo adds a nice touch of bright red fruit.

Design You won't impress anyone with this bottle. The font cheesily evokes old Europe; the bright yellow label is nicely eye-catching, though.

Carlo Rossi Paisano

Rank Unranked bargain-basement selection
Country United States **Vintage tasted** Non-vintage
Grapes Undisclosed
Drink with glazed ham, berry desserts, or in sangría
Website www.carlorossi.com

Did the Kool-Aid Man grow these grapes? Almost all of our blind tasters commented on the sugary, but not overwhelming, taste and feel of this jug wine. The admirers added that it was light, fruity, spirited, and fun. Low acidity actually defines the wine more than sugar. Regardless, it sounds like the makings of sangría to us: throw in some fresh-cut oranges, apples, and brandy. With apologies to Mr. Rossi, this is how we think the Paisano is best served.

Nose It may sound a little silly, but the wine smells a bit like grape juice, although there were other red fruits in the mix too—nothing offensive.

Mouth Tasters lauded its simplicity and chuggability. This isn't by any means the sweetest Rossi, but it still tastes like...well, sangría-to-be.

Design It's hard not to be nostalgic at the sight of a Carlo Rossi jug with its cute little carrying handle. The label design is full-out Italian-Americana, from the red, white, and green color scheme to the fat Italian(ish) man proudly displaying his grapes.

Casa Rey Malbec

Rank #17 of 135 heavy New World reds under $15 tasted
Country Argentina **Vintage tasted** 2004
Grapes Malbec
Drink with Jamaican curry, chicken mole, chiles rellenos

You hear a lot about the "up-and-coming" quality of Argentine Malbecs these days. But the only new thing about this old wine region is that the producers have finally begun exporting more. As a result, the style has turned bolder and fruitier—more "Parkerized." This wine, though, represents a happy balance between Old and New World styles. It's not as spicy or fruit-forward as some Malbecs, but it's still big and powerful, so you'll want to pair it with rich, deeply flavored foods.

Nose Sweet aromas of fresh fruit—some blind tasters identified cherry—reign here.

Mouth Hints of herbs and vegetables lurk within this somewhat thick wine.

Design A bold but pleasant burst of bright yellow has a clear indigenous fetish; if you spend a lot of time in Ten Thousand Villages stores, you'll love having this bottle on your dinner table.

Casal Garcia Vinho Verde

 $8

Rank #6 of 21 light Old World whites under $15 tasted
Country Portugal **Vintage tasted** Non-vintage
Grapes Trajadura, Loureiro, Arinto, Azal
Drink with sushi, ceviche, carpaccio, raw oysters
Website www.aveleda.pt

A bright, effervescent, summery wine, this bottle should be served at a colder temperature than non-sparkling whites. While Vinho Verde is technically not considered sparkling, there is a slight carbon-dioxide prickle. This allows it to pair easily with many different fresh, cold foods—a trick that sommeliers love to use. This could be the sushi wine to end all.

Nose There's a slight sourness here, balanced by warm notes of hay and yeast.

Mouth It's unquestionably fizzy, and some of our blind tasters found the liquid beneath the bubbles to be a bit thin. We just call it light; the alcohol's low, too.

Design The lace background and coat of arms are a bit frilly, but the designers avoid the great-aunt's-house look through decent symmetry and harmony. In multiples, the bottles make great decorations when the wine's all gone.

Castillo de Molina Pinot Noir

Viña San Pedro

Rank #3 of 52 light New World reds under $15 tasted
Country Chile **Vintage tasted** 2005
Grapes Pinot Noir
Drink with bouillabaisse, roast fish, vegetable cream soups
Website www.sanpedro.cl

Chilean wines often waver between Old World restraint and New World aggressiveness. Here we find more of the former, with a classic, precise version of Pinot Noir. The body's neither too thin nor overbearing. In fact, this wine is good served slightly chilled and can be paired even with something as light as fish.

Nose The Pinot Noir aroma, when it's done right—as it is here—is unlike any other; some people call it strawberry, but that doesn't quite capture its fresh, herbal uniqueness.

Mouth A spicy explosion of vegetal flavors is a big contrast to the nose; crisp acidity binds it together.

Design We love the elegance and balance of this well designed Burgundy-style bottle, with glints of gold on black and restrained black-and-white photo imagery combining for an expensive look.

Cave de Lugny Mâcon-Villages

$11

Rank #2 of 15 heavy Old World whites under $15 tasted
Country France **Vintage tasted** 2006
Grapes Chardonnay
Drink with cream of asparagus soup, salade niçoise
Website www.cave-lugny.com

This wine comes from an underappreciated area of Burgundy, and it's a relative steal—most white Burgundies, especially elegant ones like this, are way out of this book's price range. This is the furthest thing from an overoaked California Chardonnay. Instead, it's steely and complex, a reminder of what the Chardonnay grape is capable of when it's not hidden under layers of fake vanilla and butter.

Nose There's a lot going on here; blind tasters found it flowery, but it's also a bit metallic, with touches of green apple. One blind taster smelled brioche. Good morning.

Mouth A nice steely body of apples and lemons ends in a slightly stunted finish. After all, it is a simple table wine.

Design Classic but cheery, the label barely manages to avoid pomposity. Maybe we have extra tolerance for its eye-catching color scheme of blues and yellows—the pride of Sweden.

Cavit Merlot

$9

Rank #5 of 39 light Old World reds under $15 tasted
Country Italy **Vintage tasted** 2005
Grapes Merlot
Drink with pâté or terrine, grilled tuna, or by itself
Website www.cavitcollection.com

It's hard to find cheap, pleasant, widely available Italian reds that are free of the exaggerated barnyard aromas that tend to plague low-grade Chianti, Montepulciano d'Abruzzo, and such. This light, spicy, young, and simple bottle is the exception. Its fresh acidity—higher than in most saccharine Merlot counterparts from the other side of the pond—pleased our blind tasters, although some noticed artificial qualities as well.

Nose Blind tasters found the aromas to be a little industrial, with some finding cherry, green pepper, and cinnamon.

Mouth It's a little sour, vegetal, and peppery, and a touch more chemical than is desirable. The finish is light but satisfying.

Design The label tries—but fails—to go for a Frances Mayes-style *Under the Tuscan Sun* aesthetic, with the family farm and a haphazard mix of cheap, outdated fonts and frills.

Charles Shaw Cabernet Sauvignon

Trader Joe's "Two-Buck Chuck"

Rank Unranked bargain-basement selection
Country United States **Vintage tasted** 2004
Grapes Cabernet Sauvignon
Drink with macaroni and cheese, shepherd's pie

Two-Buck Chuck, beloved by college students and contrarian penny pinchers, has qualified for our Top 100—not because it's great, but because value counts. Many of our blind tasters found it surprisingly easy to drink—and, they imagined, easy to get drunk on, too. It's got an almost syrupy feel to it, leading us to think that this might just be what the Houston rap stars are referencing when they talk about "sizzurp." Skip the sizzurp, and sip the Shaw.

Nose There are some chemical aromas, but there's lots of easy-to-notice fruit.

Mouth It's a bit medicinal, yet you can still find some Cab character in this low-end California wine industry surplus. However, the flavors in different lots can vary. Apparently we got a good one.

Design Don't look for the words "Two-Buck Chuck" anywhere on the rote, poorly designed label; just call him Charles Shaw.

Charles Shaw Chardonnay

Trader Joe's "Two-Buck Chuck"

$3

Rank Unranked bargain-basement selection
Country United States **Vintage tasted** 2006
Grapes Chardonnay
Drink with fried fish, fried cheese

Yes, it's Two-Buck Chuck, and its reputation will always precede it. (It's actually three bucks in most of the country.) You've probably tried the Chuck at some point—even if just out of curiosity—but many of our blind tasters were shocked to find they'd preferred it to some $50 wines; nothing else in our tastings (except Dom Pérignon) incited such loud exclamations when the paper bag was ripped open. Take our opinion under advisement, however: the Two-Buck Chuck often differs in quality from one batch to the next.

Nose Tropical fruits and a synthetic twist were the most commonly identified aromas.

Mouth Many blind tasters found it a bit chemical, but most felt that it was still balanced. The finish is abrupt.

Design A seventh-grader with default Windows fonts and Microsoft Word could probably produce something similar. At least there's no outline text.

Château La Grange Clinet

$14

1er Côtes de Bordeaux

Rank #6 of 18 heavy Old World reds under $15 tasted
Country France **Vintage tasted** 2005
Grapes Merlot, Cabernet Sauvignon, Cabernet Franc
Drink with beef in wine sauce, game meats
Website www.biotope.lagrangeclinet.fr

Who wouln't want a wine like this? It's a time-frozen classic red Bordeaux that will transport you back to that first trip to Europe and that first sip of great—okay, good—wine in some cheap café. And if you've yet to make that gastronomical pilgrimage, never fear; a couple of glasses of this, and you'll be checking out flights. (These cheap Bordeaux bottles are getting expensive, but you can blame the dollar for that.) Pair it well—this is strictly a dinner wine—and you'll be in a happy place.

Nose One blind taster likened smelling this wine to walking into a cigar bar filled with men in musty cologne.

Mouth It's full of dark fruit, slightly bitter, and very French.

Design Even if you think the look is silly, it's timeless. People will think you've spent more than you really have when they see this bottle—and especially when they taste its contents.

The trials of a young winemaker
Confronting the human factors of consumer taste

As I write this, I am launching my tenth vintage on my family's estate in Provence, Le Grand Cros. When I took over, I had no experience in wine and little knowledge, so I approached my new challenge academically, like a scientist. I surrounded myself with a good team, did a master's degree at Bordeaux's prestigious ENITA, went to conferences, read books and theses, met with professors, and exchanged ideas with other producers, cellar-masters, oenologists, consultants, suppliers, and just about anyone else who would talk to me.

When I began, I had the naïve idea that if I just concentrated on making the best damn wine possible, and showed it to as many buyers and critics as possible, it would speak for itself and word would spread. As I learned the hard way, that's less than half the battle. Nowadays, most of my time and energy is devoted to trying to convince people that my wine is better than anyone else's—or, failing that, convincing them that I'm nicer, more charming, or more whatever-will-make-them-buy-wine. Although I have met some fun and interesting people in the process, I find this new job much less fulfilling.

I have come to believe that there is no universal standard for quality in wine, that taste is subjective, and that the challenge for the wine producer is not to make the best wine—for there is no such thing. Instead, we must make wine for which we can find customers. At times, this seems like an almost hopeless endeavor, because, as Robin explains in the book, most customers don't have the confidence to separate what they've been *told* to like from what they *really* like.

I have therefore decided that my next challenge will be to develop a website called tastemap.net, where I plan to establish a system that can objectively, reliably, and accurately enable wine drinkers to identify wines that they will like before they buy them. In the meantime, let's all start blind tasting. It's the best way to get in touch with our palates. –*Julian Faulkner*

Château Ste. Michelle Pinot Gris

Columbia Valley

$13

Rank #12 of 50 light New World whites under $15 tasted
Country United States (Northwest) **Vintage tasted** 2006
Grapes Pinot Gris, Viognier
Drink with crab cocktail, crawfish, grilled shrimp
Website www.ste-michelle.com

This Pinot Gris from Washington State made us—and our blind tasters—happy. It's got more character than most Italian Pinot Grigio versions, plus zippy acidity and a nice, crisp mouthfeel—so crisp that some found it to be almost prickly. It's a refreshing wine, especially on a hot day, or with a heaping plate of shellfish. There's only one thing that irks us: why can't there be more wines like this coming out of the United States?

Nose It's faint but flowery, as Pinot Gris tends to be, with an aromatic boost from Viognier. Still, many tasters liked its subtlety; if you concentrate, you'll find citrus.

Mouth Lots of tasters noticed green apple and flowers, and one person even found notes of cream soda.

Design The papery label is elegant, and the slight lifted section along the top is an interesting touch. Let's work on the froofy cursive, though.

Château Ste. Michelle Riesling

$10

Columbia Valley

Rank #2 of 51 sweet and aromatic wines under $15 tasted
Country United States (Northwest) **Vintage tasted** 2006
Grapes Riesling
Drink with Indian and Thai curries, vindaloo, jerk chicken
Website www.ste-michelle.com

You'll definitely want to drink this Riesling with food. It's not sweet enough to stand on its own as a dessert wine, yet it's too sweet to stand and sip at a bar. You'd do best to pair it with spicy dishes that would ordinarily overwhelm something less flowery. We think a dry Austrian or Alsace Riesling would be worth the extra few bucks, but many blind tasters loved this wine.

Nose It's not as aromatic as some Rieslings, and most blind tasters found the nose to be quite faint. Lemon was commonly identified.

Mouth Here the sweetness really comes on, tempered by decent acidity. The liquid feels thick and oily—even sickly to some.

Design The bright green bottle provides a punchy backdrop, but the label's pompous script reminds us of a stuffy hotel restaurant. We can't explain why the winery has chosen to misspell its own name; the circumflex is missing in the word "Château."

Château Ste. Michelle Sauvignon Blanc

$10

Columbia Valley

Rank #9 of 50 light New World whites under $15 tasted
Country United States (Northwest) **Vintage tasted** 2005
Grapes Sauvignon Blanc **Drink with** ceviche, grilled fish
Website www.ste-michelle.com

Now this is a Sauvignon Blanc. It's not as in-your-face as what you see coming out of New Zealand, and for that we like it. Some did find the wine a bit intense, but only because of the high acidity—exactly what makes it so good with citrusy food. The Pacific Northwest has ben putting out wines of increasingly consistent quality, and the region's cool climate ensures that the grapes aren't overripe or the wines too sweet.

Nose It's a pleasant mix of flowers and citrus—some blind tasters smelled tropical fruits.

Mouth It's lean, with a lot of acidity; this led some to think it would be much better when paired with food.

Design It's got that Château Ste. Michelle look: fairly classy, yet also a little old and stilted—largely because of the cursive font. Still, the paper's high quality, and it's better than looking at a brightly colored animal.

Citra Pinot Grigio

$7

Rank #9 of 21 light Old World whites under $15 tasted
Country Italy **Vintage tasted** 2005
Grapes Pinot Grigio
Drink with smoked salmon, cream soups, fish carpaccio
Website www.citrawines.com

Pinot Grigio too often tastes like nothing at all, and the light aromas and flavors of this wine left blind tasters wanting more. But if you stick your nose way into the glass, inhale deeply, and then hold the liquid in your mouth for a while, you'll get the full effect—and it's nice. This is a pleasant, if subdued, table wine, with more elegance and balance than you'll find in a lot of New World wines three or four times the price.

Nose It's faint and vague; some sensitive blind tasters identified tropical fruit. (But if you use your imagination, you can probably find tropical fruit in New York tap water.)

Mouth It comes on slightly sweet, but a healthy dose of acidity balances the effect well and leads to a harmonious finish.

Design This is one of the more modern of cheap Italian bottles; the transparent label's a nice change, but we can't endorse the attempt at minimalist painting, and the overall look is a bit trying-too-hard 1980s.

Columbia Crest
Cabernet Sauvignon
Two Vines

$8

Rank #12 of 135 heavy New World reds under $15 tasted
Country United States (Northwest) Vintage tasted 2003
Grapes Cabernet Sauvignon Drink with prime rib, sausage
Website www.columbia-crest.com

Columbia Crest is Washington State's mass-market powerhouse, with a portfolio that includes four different lines of wines, of which Two Vines is the lowest priced. (Grand Estates is also in the under-$15 bracket, with several wines around $11, but none of them made the cut.) Our blind tasters consistently preferred the Two Vines line to its more expensive counterpart, perhaps because of the relative simplicity of the wines.

Nose Blind tasters found some cooked fruit, but missing was that classic Cabernet vegetality.

Mouth It's sweeter than the nose would lead you to believe, but there's still some fruitiness here, too. You'll notice some nice herbal notes if you hold it in your mouth for a few extra seconds.

Design Columbia Crest's look is in dire need of a makeover. The stilted flowers and outdated fontage just aren't cutting it.

Concannon Petite Sirah
Limited Release

Rank #2 of 135 heavy New World reds under $15 tasted
Country United States Vintage tasted 2004
Grapes Petite Sirah
Drink with a big, fat, glistening Porterhouse steak
Website www.concannonvineyard.com

This big red wine's back label will tell you that Concannon, which was founded in 1883 "along California's Central Coast of California," was "the world's first winery to bottle Petite Sirah." It's a food wine, to be sure, and unashamed of its masculine, aggressive style. Although the price scrapes against the upper end of our spectrum, it's a better bargain if you measure by the pound—the bottle seems to weigh twice as much as others.

Nose Blind tasters found licorice and a woodsy smell.

Mouth Black pepper, solid tannins, and savory notes led our blind tasters to think this wine was far more expensive than it is.

Design This is certainly one of the heaviest bottles in the under-$15 market—and it's as pompous as it is massive, with outdated silver and grey trim, a weird raised glass logo, and that horrific hotel-restaurant script. Still, an uninformed guest could think it was a $25 wine.

Cono Sur Cabernet Sauvignon

Central Valley

Rank #11 of 135 heavy New World reds under $15 tasted
Country Chile **Vintage tasted** 2005
Grapes Cabernet Sauvignon
Drink with chili, game meats, pumpkin pie

This Chilean Cab maintains an interesting balance of sweet and spicy, although it's weighted more heavily on the sweet side of things. This led blind tasters to find it easy to drink, even by itself. Something about the wine also seems a bit reminiscent of Christmas, with a wreath of fiery, herbal aromas and tastes that turn it into a nice bottle for cold weather or the holidays.

Nose Many blind tasters smelled berries, and one even found a little mint. There isn't as much of a vegetal aspect as you'll find in many Cabs.

Mouth It comes on sweet, so if you're not a New World lover, you'll be annoyed. There are also big notes of fire and cedar underneath.

Design It's a nice color scheme, with bright red foil that's more harmonious than most, and we like the brackets, but the scribble that casually evokes the South American continent lacks elegance.

Cono Sur Pinot Noir
Central Valley

Rank #4 of 52 light New World reds under $15 tasted
Country Chile **Vintage tasted** 2006
Grapes Pinot Noir
Drink with coq au vin, roast duck, hard cheeses

It's Chilean, all right, but put it in a brown paper bag, and you'll have your tasters thinking they're drinking simple French red Burgundy—which means high acidity balancing out deeply harmonious strawberryish fruit, with perhaps a slight thinness to the liquid. Pair it with the right foods, and it blossoms. We like to drink acidic Pinot Noirs with just about anything, but you could also have fun finishing a bottle by itself—and not just because you're wasted.

Nose Aside from that classic Pinotness, blind tasters also found slightly vegetal qualities.

Mouth Heavy on strawberry, the Cono Sur smacks of Pinot Noir in a way that's rarely seen in an inexpensive New World wine.

Design A bicycle dominates the latest version of this label, which is a vast improvement. We don't quite get the bike, but it makes us want to exercise, anyway.

Cousiño Macul Riesling

Doña Isadora

$9

Rank #4 of 50 light New World whites under $15 tasted
Country Chile **Vintage tasted** 2006
Grapes Riesling
Drink with oysters, aged cheese (not together)
Website www.cousinomacul.cl

The Cousiño Macul is not your average sickly sweet, syrupy New World Riesling that's best drunk with dessert—if at all. Instead, this wine speaks softly, with delicate-if-not-very-challenging flavors, and an ideal balance between acidity and sweetness. One taster described it as the small talk of wine, but sometimes that's exactly what you want. We'll happily drink this bottle outdoors on a hot summer day, or as a complement to shellfish.

Nose A few blind tasters thought it smelled like Champagne; others found delicate citrus.

Mouth A pleasant pop of acidity is bright and cheery. Some found the faintest hint of bubbles—a prickle on the tongue—but it's not a sparkling wine.

Design The bottle, like the wine, is evocative but not overdone. The look lovingly suggests old colonial Chile; it seems not to have changed for generations, but it still works.

Crane Lake Sauvignon Blanc

$5

Rank #11 of 50 light New World whites under $15 tasted
Country United States **Vintage tasted** 2005
Grapes Sauvignon Blanc
Drink with vegetable cream soup, shrimp cocktail, tuna salad

The outstanding value notwithstanding, there was almost unanimous consensus that this wine's simple, clean demeanor makes it easy to like. It's somewhat subdued for a Sauvignon Blanc, with a fainter-than-usual nose and basic fruit flavors. Don't expect fireworks, but for the price of a couple of beers, it's hard to go wrong with this refreshing bottle to complement an afternoon snack or light dinner.

Nose Blind tasters found it to be fairly faint, with a bit of fruit and even some floral notes.

Mouth Citrus flavors—lime in particular—were found by most blind tasters.

Design Crane Lake is an object lesson in how to make a cheap wine look classy: the parchment effect isn't over the top, and the well-balanced label doesn't talk down to you. The overall effect is that of a $30 or $40 wine.

Dom Pérignon Cuvée
Moët & Chandon

$150

Rank #17 of 27 sparkling wines tasted overall
Country France **Vintage tasted** 1999
Grapes Pinot Noir, Chardonnay
Drink with people who are impressed by expensive things
Website www.domperignon.com

Even if this famous Champagne were being sold for one-tenth its $150 price, it wouldn't have made our top 100 wines. It has a classic expensive Champagne taste: toasty, creamy, and earthy, with fine, restrained bubbles. The problem is, a lot of our blind tasters didn't actually like that taste. Even the wine experts that liked the wine didn't value it at anywhere near $150. For everyday wine drinkers, the Dom might be the most spectacular special-occasion rip-off in the store.

Nose If you use your imagination, it's not hard to see how those overwhelming aromas of cream and toast can turn ugly for some.

Mouth The unusual intensity is pleasant to some, not to others.

Design The pompous label maximizes the placebo effect. Why donate $150 to help float LVMH's ostentatious marketing budget?

Domaine Ste. Michelle Brut
Columbia Valley Sparkling Wine

Rank #1 of 22 sparkling wines under $15 tasted
Country United States (Northwest) **Vintage tasted** NV
Grapes Chardonnay, Pinot Noir
Drink with smoked salmon, artichokes, chocolate cake
Website www.domaine-ste-michelle.com

The darling of our blind sparkling wine tastings, Domaine Ste. Michelle routinely beat out French champagnes—two-thirds of tasters preferred it to the $150 bottle of Dom Pérignon. Why? Well, it's made in the traditional method of Champagne, and the grapes are from Washington's Columbia Valley, whose climate is similar to that of the Champagne region in France. However, the style is fresher and lighter than Champagne, and you're not paying for millions of dollars in PR stunts and glossy magazine ads featuring scantily-clad supermodels.

Nose Our blind tasters almost unanimously agreed that the nose was dominated by apples, with a bit of minerality and chalkiness.

Mouth The appliness continues, turning the mouth almost cidery for some. The finish is fresh and dry.

Design With its outdated Optima font and out-of-place swirls, the bottle looks a little cheap—but then again, it is. Thankfully.

Fâmega Vinho Verde

$7

Rank #10 of 21 light Old World whites under $15 tasted
Country Portugal **Vintage tasted** 2006
Grapes Alvarinho
Drink with sushi, spicy raw fish dishes, or by itself

There are some great wines coming out of Portugal at all price levels, but sadly, not many of them are distributed widely enough for inclusion in *The Wine Trials*. The exception is Vinho Verde, the almost-sparkling "green" wine that represents one of the gustatory world's most unsung values. This one is effervescent and lively, with extremely high acidity. Just make sure you serve it cold (even over ice, if you prefer); warm Vinho Verde is pretty much undrinkable.

Nose It's very refreshing, with some crisp, clean apple and citrus; it reminded one blind taster of lemon sherbet.

Mouth It's got more carbon dioxide than most Vinho Verde. Some blind tasters also found the taste to be metallic.

Design The Trajan font's not bad, but as far as the image goes, these designers should be banned from using the Photoshop "Filters" menu.

Fat Bastard Chardonnay

Thierry and Guy

$11

Rank #4 of 15 heavy Old World white wines
Country France **Vintage tasted** 2005
Grapes Chardonnay
Drink with Indian curries, creamy soups
Website www.fatbastardwine.com

Why? Why call a wine Fat Bastard? There's the obvious answer that seeing the "critter wine" revolution and raising it to vulgarity would help to sell bottles. (Which, unfortunately, it probably does.) Thierry & Guy's official explanation is that it's a reference to the big, round body of the wine. We admit that the liquid does have a nice thickness to it, even if it lacks the steely subtlety of better French Chardonnay. If the name bothers you, just wrap the bottle in a brown paper bag. That's what we did.

Nose Hints of flowers and sweetness make the nose a crowd-pleaser, but it's not very complex.

Mouth Surprise, surprise: at 13.5% alcohol, it's big, especially for a French white. And fat.

Design The label sags under the weight of a seemingly sated hippo— the fat bastard, we presume. It's worthy of a grin. The simplicity and use of white space is nice, too.

Fetzer Valley Oaks Merlot

Rank #5 of 52 light New World reds under $15 tasted
Country United States **Vintage tasted** 2005
Grapes Merlot
Drink with roast chicken, smothered pork chops
Website www.fetzer.com

It's not a typical, overdone California Merlot, and for that we—and our blind tasters—love this wine; a certain light-handedness turns the Fetzers more complex than the competition. It doesn't whack you over the head with oak or sweet, rotting fruit, and even if there's little complexity, the wine is easy to drink. We've been surprised, in these tastings, to find several cheap California Merlots we can recommend; perhaps the *Sideways*-fueled Merlot recession has forced quality up.

Nose Straightforward and simple. There are pleasant berry aromas; some blind tasters found a bit of woodsiness.

Mouth American Merlot that it is, it flirts with sweetness, although we also found chocolate and vegetal notes.

Design Fetzer labels are just too busy for us. Do they really need a foil stamp over the vineyard? And the pompous script is outdated.

Feudi di San Gregorio Falanghina

Sannio

$14

WINNER

Rank #1 of 21 light Old World whites under $15 tasted
Country Italy **Vintage tasted** 2005
Grapes Falanghina
Drink with whole roasted or grilled fish
Website www.feudi.it

When people talk about southern Italy these days, you always hear about concentrated reds like Primitivo. Close your ears and check out this underrated, indigenous white from old-school Campania. Falanghina is delicious with food, and this one comes in one of the most elegantly designed bottles in Italy. Our blind tasters loved the perky flavors and relentless but balanced acidity. At $14, stock up—especially before the dollar gets any weaker. And drink it soon.

Nose Restrained floral notes are part of this wine's delicate balance; nothing jumps out at you.

Mouth Lightly fruity, it's got an acidic kick to it, but it is by no means overpowering. The finish seemed tart to some tasters, but in a good way.

Design The double square against tapered glass is an achievement of modern wine art. We've seen $300 bottles that don't look nearly this good.

Freixenet Cordon Negro Brut

Rank #2 of 22 sparkling wines under $15 tasted
Country Spain **Vintage tasted** Non-vintage
Grapes Macabeo, Xarel-lo, Parellada
Drink with vegetable or shrimp tempura, smoked fish
Website www.freixenet.com

Freixenet plays off of all the sparkling wine stereotypes out there. The website would have you believe that only dangerously attractive young people drink it while celebrating a massive bonus or entertaining celebrities at a bottle-service nightclub. But don't fear; there's no Freixenet rule again frumpy or non-celebratory drinkers. On the contrary: anyone who knows this delicious sparkler will also know how cheap it is. Not that there's anything wrong with that.

Nose There's a nice balance here between fruit and a sort of buttered-bread smell.

Mouth Tasters were least impressed by the aftertaste, with some calling it metallic, but they loved the bubbles' smoothness.

Design The solid black bottles are unique; the gold must, at least, excite all the chromatic minimalists out there.

Freixenet Cordon Negro Extra Dry $9

Rank #8 of 22 sparkling wines under $15 tasted
Country Spain **Vintage tasted** Non-vintage
Grapes Macabeo, Xarel-lo, Parellada
Drink with eggs benedict, bagels and lox, or in a mimosa
Website www.freixenet.com

Quick wine lesson: if you like your sparkling wines dry, you'd love them extra dry, right? Wrong. Brut is actually the driest classification, so only go for the Extra Dry if you like them a little sweeter. Lesson #2: Know how to pronounce Freixenet? Neither did we. Turns out it's "fresh-eh-net" (the word is Catalán, as this wine is from Catalunya in Northeastern Spain). It's a brunch wine, and it also works well with slightly spicy foods, as the sweetness creates a balance—if not as nice as the balance of the Brut.

Nose It's a mix of fruitiness with some floral notes.

Mouth It's sweeter than the Freixenet Brut, to be sure, with hints of apple. However, some blind tasters felt that it still wasn't as sweet as other producers' versions of Extra Dry.

Design The extremely dark Freixenet bottle mysteriously conceals its contents. Some people probably buy it out of mere curiosity.

Full Circle Zinfandel

Rank #8 of 135 heavy New World reds under $15 tasted
Country United States **Vintage tasted** 2003
Grapes Zinfandel
Drink with oven-roasted chicken and potatoes

Organic perishables have become very fashionable of late. No one wants to say no to an earth-friendly and health-friendly product—yet few people want to pay twice as much for organic. This Zin is the exception: it's reasonably priced, and the taste doesn't seem to suffer from the lack of sulfur, a frequent problem with organics. Its muted mint and chocolate flavors are more pleasant than they are in most Zins.

Nose It's a dark wine with aromas of cherry and raspberry, and that so-called "international" (or fruit-forward) smell.

Mouth Noticeable tannins combine with dark chocolate, coffee, black cherry, and vanilla, and it all wraps up with a menthol finish.

Design Circles that bear a faint resemblance to grapes are reminiscent of childhood doodles, and the bright blue on the neck of the bottle is an amusing diversion. It's a pleasant, playful bottle.

Gato Negro Sauvignon Blanc

Viña San Pedro

$6

Rank #7 of 50 light New World whites under $15 tasted
Country Chile **Vintage tasted** 2006
Grapes Sauvignon Blanc
Drink with simple salads, green fruit, or as an apéritif
Website www.sanpedro.cl

This Chilean Sauvignon Blanc is in stark contrast to the Sauvignon Blancs you see coming out of New Zealand. It's got a more muted style, with more complexity. "Cat pee" is one of the classic flavors that the wine establishment recognizes in Sauvignon Blanc (this is meant in the best possible sense). But we also find some exciting floral notes. Blind tasters loved the acidity—which is crisp without spinning out of control—and the refreshing finish.

Nose We found lots of fruit, especially lime, as well as tiny hints of flowers; it reminded one blind taster of springtime.

Mouth It's quite expansive, and the acidity isn't overdone. We found more flowers here, too.

Design The capital-letter-in-the-middle contraction "GatoNegro" feels very 1980s, but the gold-on-black San Pedro logo and black cat are strangely appealing.

Georges Duboeuf
Beaujolais-Villages

Rank #7 of 39 light Old World reds under $15 tasted
Country France Vintage tasted 2006
Grapes Gamay
Drink with pesto, spicy salads, a picnic with bread and cheese
Website www.duboeuf.com

Beaujolais-Villages, one of Burgundy's humblest appellations, steadily produces wine that's light, fruity, cheap, and pleasant, if not earth-shattering. It's the kind of wine you can buy in a French supermarket for a couple of Euros and have a fantastic lunch of cheese, baguette, and wine on a park bench. What's sad, however, is that nowadays the price of French wine is going up so fast that even the basic Beaujolais is starting to move out of the affordable range for many everyday wine drinkers.

Nose It's not very intense, but nonetheless, it's pleasant. Some tasters called it nutty.

Mouth Tasters found it fruity with a slight touch of bitterness and astringent acidity.

Design Of the Duboeuf bottles, this one is the least offensive to the eye. But that's not saying much. Other designs include a denim bottle and one with brightly colored splashes far more garish than these flowers.

Geyser Peak Sauvignon Blanc $10

Rank #14 of 50 light New World whites under $15 tasted
Country United States **Vintage tasted** 2006
Grapes Sauvignon Blanc
Drink with fish tacos, shrimp or vegetable tempura
Website www.geyserpeakwinery.com

Geyser Peak's proclaimed dedication to terroir (see, e.g., their website) is relatively unique at this price point among American producers. It's refreshing to see such a commitment coming from a winery that's churning out hundreds of thousands of cases of wine each year. Whether or not the locavorous claim is hollow, our blind tasters liked this wine. It's a bright, summery drink, fit for outdoor entertaining or indoor imbibing.

Nose Fresh citrus—grapefruit in particular—dominates the nose.

Mouth The effect is pleasant, with a nice finish and enjoyable, but not overwhelming, acidity. Some blind tasters detected a bit of prickle.

Design Too many wine designers cave in to the temptation to throw in a château or some curlique vines. They should take a lesson from Geyser Peak on keeping it simple.

Grand Pacific Starliner White

$12

Rutherford Wine Company

Rank #4 of 51 sweet and aromatic wines under $15 tasted
Country United States Vintage tasted 2005
Grapes Chardonnay, Sauvignon Blanc, Muscat Canelli
Drink with chocolate cake, fruit plate
Website www.rutherfordwine.com

We tasted 10 different Rutherford wines, but this was the only one that ended up making it into the book. Here, the Muscat grape turns the wine quite sugary, so you'll like it if you grew up drinking soda and don't generally like wine. On the other hand, we would enjoy it with dessert; what's strange is that wines like this don't really warn you of their sweetness on the label. That's how sweet the mainstream has become. One taster noted that her 15-year-old would love it. Is this *The Wine Trials'* first kid-friendly wine?

Nose You know you're in for something saccharine by the scent alone; blind tasters smelled banana.

Mouth A creeping sweetness builds upon itself the longer you keep it in your mouth.

Design The old-school train conjures up exciting images of cross-country trips, and the golden yellow looks good with the maroon text. It's a fun label.

Guigal Côtes du Rhône

Rank #2 of 18 heavy Old World reds under $15 tasted
Country France **Vintage tasted** 2004
Grapes Syrah, Grenache, Mourvèdre
Drink with roast turkey with stuffing and gravy, veal stew
Website www.guigal.com

When we think of wine, we still think of France. Cheap French wines, although they're getting more expensive every year in dollar terms, are still often a better value than their cheap New World counterparts. Guigal is a producer popularized by Robert Parker, so you won't be surprised by the big fruit on the nose and mouth. It's versatile, and can be drunk with myriad foods.

Nose Fruity aromas are definitely there, and you might find spices, too.

Mouth It's very big on flavor—and everything else, for that matter. Tasters found substantial tannnins and alcohol. Some even said that the finish burned a bit.

Design The bottle is an amusing mix of old-school French fontage with the new-school desire to evoke a sense of place through nostalgic geographical imagery.

Harlow Ridge Pinot Grigio

$10

Rank #6 of 50 light New World whites under $15 tasted
Country United States **Vintage tasted** 2005
Grapes Pinot Grigio
Drink with fried calamari, white pizza, cream soup

This is the type of wine that would be easy to overlook on trip after trip to the supermarket; it's got that cheap, generic California look and name. Ignore the package, though, and you've got a wonderful wine. It's complex; several blind tasters compared the yeasty nose to Champagne, and almost all lauded the wine's lovely balance. You wouldn't want to show up at a dinner party with this garish bottle, though; you're better off brown-bagging it.

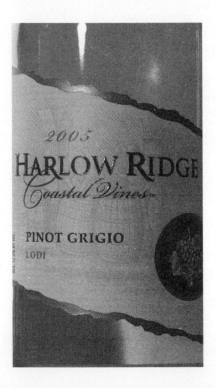

Nose Blind tasters were wowed by the delicate hints of fresh grass, citrus, and pear on the nose.

Mouth Lots of citrus drive the eminently enjoyable flavors; the finish is alcoholic but refreshing.

Design The look is a train wreck, from the cheap ripped-label effect to a shadowed font with the aesthetic of a cheap Italian-American restaurant. The grape is spelled "Pinot Grigo" on the back label. Enough said.

House Wine
The Magnificent Wine Company

$12

Rank #3 of 135 heavy New World reds under $15 tasted
Country United States (Northwest) **Vintage tasted** 2005
Grapes Cabernet Sauvignon, Merlot, Syrah, Malbec
Drink with steak au poivre and fries, osso buco
Website www.magnificentwine.com

Were it not for brown bags, we probably never would have tried this wine; a lot of these new trying-too-hard labels tend to suggest sugary plonk. Not here: this is a Washington State beauty. From start to finish, House Wine drinks like a big, elegant Old World food wine—and one that's closer to $100 than the $12 you'll pay for this one. At this price, it's a gift.

Nose Some blind tasters found it a little bit stinky, Old-World-style, though it's got some nice cooked red fruit. Others found leathery and earthy aromas.

Mouth It's beautiful: a dead ringer for a high-priced Bordeaux, but with less astringency than you'd find in France, so it's ready to drink now.

Design Perhaps it's the Magic Marker-style aesthetic that's scaring restaurants away from actually pouring this as their house wine. Why must this producer sell itself so short? On the other hand, they know more about wine sales than we do.

The trials of pouring
A sommelier's open letter to customers everywhere

I would like to start by thanking you for choosing wine. You've just done every winemaker, importer, and sommelier in the country a huge favor, and you have our heartfelt gratitude. Although wine has been at the American table for a while (Thomas Jefferson was a big oenophile), it has only recently begun to surpass beer and liquor in sales.

In truth, most professional sommeliers privately scoff at the bottles of Cavit overflowing in the grocery store wine aisle, as well as many of the other brands mentioned in this book; we would much rather introduce you to the latest obscure Italian grape variety. However, these wines happen to make up a huge part of America's market. They're also the potential stepping stones toward the more wine-savvy, curious public that sommeliers dream of. After all, sommeliers right now are asking, "How can I get them to drink good Grüner Veltliner?" Yet it is apparent we still have to address the more basic question: "How can I get them to drink Grüner Veltliner?"

So, drink up, but I'd like to request a few small favors:

• Drop the words "dry" and "sweet" from your vocabulary when describing your tastes to a sommelier. Instead, describe the fruit flavors you like in wine, or better yet, refer to a wine you have enjoyed lately.

• Forget the ice bucket. A white wine hits its stride aromatically between 45 and 55 degrees.

• Fear not acidity and tannins. There's too much "jammy," "lush," and "soft" stuff around. Wine needs balance. Acid is the skeletal system of a wine, tannin the muscular.

• Always play around. Why not match Prosecco with sorbet? Oloroso Sherry with a ribeye? Who cares? The fun of wine is in its—and your palate's—diversity.

–Nat Davis

Huber Hugo Grüner Veltliner $12

Rank #3 of 21 light Old World whites under $15 tasted
Country Austria **Vintage tasted** 2005
Grapes Grüner Veltliner
Drink with grilled fish, potatoes au gratin, sea scallops

Unfortunately, so few dry German or Austrian wines are widely available in the US that almost none made our top 100. For starters, most cheap wines coming out of Northern Europe are sickly sweet (think Blue Nun Liebfraumilch). Beautiful, crisp, dry Rieslings are out there, but their price points are well above our cut-off. On the other hand, we'll happily point you in the direction of this easy-to-find Grüner Veltliner, a beautifully dry, restrained wine that's all about crisp acidity and precise flavors.

Nose It's only slightly floral; the main flavor you'll pick up on is citrus. Serve it colder than most.

Mouth Refreshingly high acidity is the earmark, but a nice, long finish is a welcome surprise.

Design These painfully hip, retro labels, with their bright stripes, make this bottle a nice centerpiece for a mod dinner party. Austin Powers would shag to this bottle.

Jindalee Estate Rosé

$7

Rank #3 of 29 rosés under $15 tasted
Country Australia Vintage tasted 2006
Grapes Shiraz
Drink with pulled pork and slaw, spicy Indian dishes
Website www.jindaleewines.com.au

For a wine whose producer describes its style as "fruit-driven," this dry rosé is pleasantly balanced. It's got a big, alcoholic feel to it, but it isn't a classic new-school Australia-California-style fruit bomb. It is still on the sweet side of things, so it would be best to drink it with something big and spicy. Or, if you prefer, drink it on its own; it could almost stand alone as a feminine cocktail. Whatever you do, you must chill it well—otherwise it's terrible. For a morbid laugh, visit the website, which features a naked man in a tub of grape must.

Nose If you close your eyes, you might imagine that this is a white wine, with its delicate aromas.

Mouth A silky mouthfeel with red fruit pleased blind tasters.

Design A disaster. The 1980s color scheme is rather off-putting, especially when zig-zaggingly applied to the emu. And the jarringly purple label totally clashes with its pink contents.

Kettmeir Pinot Grigio

Vigneti delle Dolomiti

Rank #4 of 21 light Old World whites under $15 tasted
Country Italy **Vintage tasted** 2006
Grapes Pinot Grigio
Drink with green salad with goat cheese, garlicky shrimp
Website www.kettmeir.com

It makes us happy that we can include this wine from Alto Adige in northern Italy, because few wines from that breathtakingly beautiful region, in the foothills of the Dolomites, meet the under-$15 criterion. The Kettmeir is representative of the region: bright and exciting, a bit flowery, a bit citrusy, and pleasantly acidic. With supremely modern facilities, Alto Adige is the pride of the Italian wine industry at the moment, eclipsing the offerings that have been coming in from giants Cavit and Mezzacorona in nearby Trentino.

Nose Blind tasters found a bit of everything from flowers and bright herbal notes to lovely citrus aromas.

Mouth It's refreshing, with just the right amount of natural acidity and a nice finish, as well as pear, apple, and lemon.

Design
Although the label is clearly the benefactor of some real graphic design, this bottle isn't terribly exciting. The text is stylish enough, but the pink granite color verges on sickly.

Kiwi Cuvée

Underdog Wine Merchants

Rank #7 of 21 light Old World whites under $15 tasted
Country France **Vintage tasted** 2006
Grapes Sauvignon Blanc
Drink with cheese plate, seared sea scallops
Website www.underdogwinemerchants.com

These sorts of Old-New World hybrids are rapidly springing up these days, and this is one of their more successful marriages. Don't be deceived by the "Kiwi" designation: the wine is from France—made with Sauvignon Blanc grapes from the Jardin de la France in the Loire Valley—and not from New Zealand. Although two tasters identified Champagne-like flavors, this one's ultimately a simple crowd pleaser for a party.

Nose It seems to smell cleaner the more you sniff it.

Mouth With some earthy fruit, the Kiwi didn't make our tasters swoon. One compared it to a lover who doesn't abuse you, but the sex isn't great.

Design The bottle, like the wine, combines Old World simplicity with New World marketing. The latter, perhaps, is represented merely by a golden, new-agey swirl that we don't quite get. But we'll take this over a critter wine any day.

ADD

La Vieille Ferme Rouge
Perrin & Fils

$8

Rank #3 of 18 heavy Old World reds under $15 tasted
Country France **Vintage tasted** 2005
Grapes Grenache, Syrah, Carignan, Cinsault
Drink with cassoulet, pot roast
Website www.lavieilleferme.com

This screwcap wine, which comes from a humble pocket of the Rhône Valley called Côtes du Ventoux, has that lovely, soft, fruity-but-not-sweet style characteristic of Grenache from southern France. This is the kind of simple but enjoyable Old World wine that, even with the skyrocketing Euro, still feels like a better value than anything similar coming out of the United States. Why can't we do better?

Nose Although it's faint, there's some jamminess and candied fruit. Breathe too deeply and you might get a slight chemical whiff.

Mouth The flavors include sweet spices and a slight herbal aspect. On the finish, some blind tasters found dark chocolate.

Design Don't be fooled by the fake French handwriting or the homeliness of the chicken couple flirting on the bottle: the maverick marketing punch of Perrin, the Rhône giant, is behind this big brand.

LAN Rioja Crianza
Bodegas LAN

$12

WINNER

Rank #1 of 39 light Old World reds under $15 tasted
Country Spain **Vintage tasted** 2004
Grapes Tempranillo
Drink with lamb or vegetable tagine, grilled sausage
Website www.bodegaslan.com

Rioja is the crusty old man of European wine regions. We mean that in the very best sense: most Rioja producers haven't yet caved in to the "Parkerization" of wines as some other European producers are starting to do, even in Spain and France. Love it or hate it, you'll never forget a Rioja once you've had one: it's soft and modest at first, then earthy and evocative. It is the kind of wine that creeps up on you—in every sense: it's easy to go through several bottles, too.

Nose One taster was overtaken by nostalgia from the earthy, almost musty aromas. There's some cherry, too, and what one imaginative taster described as pumpkin bread.

Mouth Many of the same flavors are here that are in the nose, with the addition of some vanilla.

Design Distressed yellow paper creates a nice backdrop for the royal red text. It definitely looks dated, but then, so is the region, and we're not complaining.

Liberty School Cabernet Sauvignon $14

Rank #5 of 135 heavy New World reds under $15 tasted
Country United States **Vintage tasted** 2005
Grapes Cabernet Sauvignon
Drink with strip steak, creamed spinach, chocolate cake
Website www.treana.com

Liberty School is a relatively humble California producer whose marketing and PR are refreshingly elementary. You've probably seen these bottles everywhere, but not in that in-your-face, Yellow Tail-ish sort of way. Rather, Liberty School makes only three wines, and the company seems to focus more resources and effort on making them well than on telling you how great they are. The Cabernet Sauvignon is the best of the Liberty School bunch, gracefully blending spices, dark fruits, and deep, seductive flavors of dark chocolate.

Nose It flirts with being too jammy, with some blind tasters calling it sweet, but for most, it doesn't quite go overboard. This is a California Cabernet, after all.

Mouth Chocolate and black pepper wooed our blind tasters.

Design Simple and relatively understated, it could easily pass for a more expensive bottle. Just as it did in a brown bag.

Lois Grüner Veltliner

Loimer

Rank #5 of 21 light Old World whites under $15 tasted
Country Austria Vintage tasted 2006
Grapes Grüner Veltliner
Drink with fresh fruit, tuna carpaccio, vegetables and dip

If you're used to thinking of Austrian and German wines as sweet, it's time for a new paradigm. Dry Austrian wines like this Grüner can be brilliant: they're not fortified with sugar, as some of those cheap wines are, so there's no artificial boost in sweetness or alcohol. This wine sticks more closely to nature's plan for the region: the cool weather keeps it crisp and bone-dry, with a pale, almost green color, and alcohol below 12%. It's a great outdoor or summer wine, and it pairs well with just about anything.

Nose You'll find somewhat faint floral and citrusy aromas.

Mouth It's all about the crisp acidity here; there are bright flavors of lime and pepper, and a noticeable tartness.

Design Ever cooler than us, the Austrians are creating some cutting-edge wine labels these days. This one is yellow, minimalist, and vaguely Sci-Fi. We think it works.

Grüner Veltliner

Lois

Lorikeet Brut

$9

Rank #4 of 22 sparkling wines under $15 tasted
Country Australia **Vintage tasted** Non-vintage
Grapes Pinot Noir, Chardonnay
Drink with good company and a cheese plate—or wedding cake

This wine is all about partying. Fruity and fun, it was seen by our blind tasters as being particularly good for toasting with. So raise your glasses to this unique product of Australia—not exactly a land known for its sparkling wine production. Many tasters also said they would happily chug it as a cold drink on a hot day. Maybe that's because of the soda-like quality; there's some noticeable sugar. Lorikeet also makes a sparkling Shiraz, but we recommend that you stick with our blind tasters and stay away from that purple, fizzy monstrosity.

Nose It's got a fruity bouquet with strong hints of cherry.

Mouth It's not so brut, really; many tasters found sweetness here.

Design Needs toning down; this is label design at its worst. Brightly colored brush strokes make up the larger part of a lorikeet, and six different fonts and sizes don't help.

Louis Latour Le Pinot Noir

Bourgogne

Rank #4 of 39 light Old World reds under $15 tasted
Country France **Vintage tasted** 2006
Grapes Pinot Noir
Drink with split pea soup, pork chops, boiled meats
Website www.louislatour.com

Many everyday wine drinkers say they like Pinot Noir—*Sideways* surely played a role in that—but fewer say they like red Burgundy, which is made with the same grape. (That's likely because French wines are much harder to find in this price range.) Back in the day, wines were known by where they came from, not by their grapes. Americans pretty much invented grape-variety labeling, and it's a sign of American pressure on the French wine industry that Louis Latour has to call their Burgundy a Pinot Noir in order to sell bottles in America. Luckily, this bottle still tastes French, not New World. It's great for a casual dinner party.

Nose Our tasters picked up on cherries and black tea. It's marked by pretty classic French Pinot aromas.

Mouth It's a bit short, full of red fruit and good acidity. This is a nice, simple table wine.

Design We're not huge fans of the script logo, but at least there are no goofy animals or vulgar names here.

Malenchini Chianti

Colli Fiorentini

$10

Rank #11 of 39 light Old World reds under $15 tasted
Country Italy **Vintage tasted** 2006
Grapes Sangiovese, Canaiolo
Drink with spaghetti alla bolognese, roast chicken, game birds

On the whole, our blind tasters had a tough time with Chianti. They tasted a lot, and liked only a few. In particular, people reacted negatively to a mulchy, almost dirty smell that the wine often gives off. It's that certain scent associated with Chianti; in wine jargon it's described as "barnyard." Some people like it, but those who hate it, *hate it*. It's here, but in unusually mild form; more obvious are the notes of fresh earth, cherries, and berries. The combination of tannins and fruit will allow this wine to age for a few years.

Nose It doesn't give much, but there's some earthiness, and what one blind taster likened to driving down a dusty road.

Mouth Within the first few minutes of opening, this wine is a bit too tannic and challenging. It'll come around, though, and it's well worth the wait.

Design The look of the label is simple and relatively inoffensive, with an old-school open face font and a yellow-and-black color scheme that makes you think of bumblebees.

Mark West Pinot Noir

$11

WINNER

Rank #1 of 52 light New World reds under $15 tasted
Country United States **Vintage tasted** 2005
Grapes Pinot Noir
Drink with roast chicken, spaghetti alla carbonara
Website www.markwestwines.com

We loved this classic Pinot in a brown bag, and the placebo effect made us love it even more after we visited the Mark West website, which outlines their simple cause (good, affordable Pinot Noir—not Merlot) in the form of a not-so-communist manifesto. It's a small operation—only nine people—and the funds are focused where they should be: in the winemaking. "Pinot for the People"? Melodramatic, perhaps, but we're definitely on board.

Nose There was no question among our tasters that there were strong cherry aromas.

Mouth Blind tasters liked its little bit of spice and strawberries. Some wished it had a slightly fuller body to support such big flavors, but we loved it for its elegant softness.

Design The playfulness of the website doesn't translate to the bottle, which is all business and tasteful design, with soothing maroons and a restrained touch of gold.

Marqués de Cáceres Rioja

Rank #1 of 15 heavy Old World whites under $15 tasted
Country Spain **Vintage tasted** 2006
Grapes Viura
Drink with macaroni and cheese, risotto
Website www.marquesdecaceres.com

Everybody knows Marqués de Cáceres, either in its white, red, or pink form; it might well be the most widely distributed Spanish brand in the US. (Keep an eye out, and you might even find it somewhere as unlikely as a gas station, drugstore, or neighborhood bodega.) Our blind tasters liked everything from Marqués de Cáceres, but the white was a true standout. It's light enough to pair with something as delicate as raw fish, but we recommend drinking it with something more substantial and flavorful. It's also good by itself; the fresh fruit flavors work their magic alone.

Nose Tasters found the aromas to be a bit floral, with touches of minerality.

Mouth Tropical fruit—banana in particular—was commonly noticed in this refreshing mouthful.

Design It's a simple, inoffensive screwcap bottle, although the design is getting old. The Marqués look works better for red wines.

Marqués de Cáceres Rioja Crianza

Rank #3 of 39 light Old World reds under $15 tasted
Country Spain **Vintage tasted** 2003
Grapes Tempranillo, Garnacha, Graciano
Drink with hearty soups, hard cheeses
Website www.marquesdecaceres.com

Rioja is all about patience. A Gran Reserva, for instance, will have been aged for five years at a minimum before it's available anywhere. Crianza, the classification of this wine, means that it has spent at least two years in cask and bottle before its release; Marqués usually waits about four, and the waiting isn't over there. You have to wait about an hour after you've opened one of these bottles for its flavors to open up. But when they do, the wine is transportative.

Nose At first it seems chemical and off-putting; give it some time, though, and it comes on with a deep, fruity, earthy nose.

Mouth It's a traditional Rioja, expansive but not overwhelming, with dark red fruit and sour cherry.

Design The aesthetic is pleasant in that nostalgic sort of way; like the style of winemaking, this bottle design hasn't changed for decades. The dark red and gold trim seem to hint at petty nobility.

Marqués de Riscal Rioja Rosé

$10

Rank #2 of 29 rosés under $15 tasted
Country Spain **Vintage tasted** 2005
Grapes Tempranillo
Drink with grilled calamari, crab salad
Website www.marquesderiscal.com

Rosé is *the* ultimate summer wine—light, refreshing, and almost too easy to drink. If you live somewhere hot, we recommend buying cases of rosé at a time, not bottles. And we're talking about dry rosé here, not blush wine from a jug. This Spanish rosé from Rioja maintains the perfect balance between fresh fruity flavors and acidity. It'll be even better with seafood—preferably seaside. (Marqués de Riscal makes some nice red Riojas, too.)

Nose Faint, fruity, and fresh aromas made our blind tasters happy.

Mouth You'll taste lots of strawberry, the characteristic flavor of the Tempranillo grape. Then you'll taste it again. And before you notice, the bottle will be gone.

Design What's unique about these old-school bottles is the gold netting that surrounds them. The system was originally used to prevent counterfeiting; if the net was broken, you knew the wine wasn't original.

Mavrodaphne of Patras
Kourtaki

$9

Rank #3 of 51 sweet and aromatic wines under $15 tasted
Country Greece **Vintage tasted** Non-vintage
Grapes Mavrodaphne
Drink with crème brûlée, strawberries
Website www.nestorimports.com

We imagine this is what sweet wine tasted like a thousand years ago. A slight deliberate oxidization means that you can keep the bottle open for a few days and the wine won't change—something you'd have to be crazy to attempt with most non-fortified wines. Otherwise, the Mavrodaphne displays all the characteristics our blind tasters were looking for in a good dessert wine: it tastes pleasantly rustic, with layers of flavors, the hot burn of alcohol, and a big, belly-satisfying sweetness.

Nose It smacks of caramel, chocolate, and nuts—not things you'd normally expect to smell in a red wine.

Mouth The sweetness, alcohol, and oxidization almost trick you into thinking this is a Port wine.

Design It's all cheesy Grecophilia, from the fonts to the gold medallion—can they be serious? At least the balance of white, red, black, and gold is soothing.

Morro Bay Cabernet Sauvignon

$10

Rank #6 of 135 heavy New World reds under $15 tasted
Country United States **Vintage tasted** 2003
Grapes Cabernet Sauvignon
Drink with steak, game meats, Mexican food

This California Cab is a pleasant surprise. Sure, it's got all those big flavors you associate with wine coming out of California, but they're not so big as to be troublesome. (We once had a problem with California Zinfandels at a blind tasting; the Zins were so overextracted that they were staining tasters' glasses, rendering them inoperative.) This wine, on the other hand, is thankfully subdued; it pairs well with meat at a dinner party.

Nose Many of our blind tasters found aromas of chocolate, along with a typical Cabernet nose.

Mouth It's a big wine, with noticeable tannins. Blind tasters also identified black fruit and wood. It's a classic but balanced Cab, and it tastes more expensive than it is.

Design
Although we like the ridged texture, this bottle's nothing special otherwise. It conveys just the info you need. Put it in a brown bag, though, and you won't care.

Brutally honest restaurant guides from Fearless Critic Media available or coming soon at local bookstores, amazon.com, and fearlesscritic.com

Fearless Critic Houston restaurant guide

Robin Goldstein, Justin Yu, Alexis Herschkowitsch, and local undercover chefs rate and review more than 400 places to eat in the greater Houston, Texas area.

Fearless Critic Austin restaurant guide

Robin Goldstein, Rebecca Markovits, and Monika Powe Nelson rate and review more than 400 places to eat in the greater Austin, Texas area.

Fearless Critic New Haven restaurant guide

Robin Goldstein, Clare Murumba, and a team of local food critics rate and review more than 300 places to eat in the New Haven, Connecticut area. Formerly known as *The Menu*.

Fearless Critic Washington DC restaurant guide

Robin Goldstein, Coco Krumme, and local undercover chefs rate and review more than 400 places to eat in the greater Washington, DC area, including Alexandria and Arlington, Virginia, and Bethesda and Chevy Chase, Maryland.

Fearless Critic Dallas-Fort Worth restaurant guide

Robin Goldstein, local food critics, and undercover chefs rate and review more than 400 places to eat in the DFW metroplex, including Addison, Irving, and Plano, Texas.

Morro Bay Chardonnay

$10

Rank #2 of 89 heavy New World whites under $15 tasted
Country United States **Vintage tasted** 2006
Grapes Chardonnay
Drink with roasted fish, lobster roll

California Chardonnay often suffers from over-oaking. In cheap wines, oak chips are often added to synthesize the toasty vanilla character that a lot of wine critics and magazines started raving about (and then consumers started craving) in the 1990s. This is nothing like your classic overoaked California Chardonnay. Rather, our blind tasters were all huge fans of this wine's ideal balance between aromas and flavors, sugars and acids; it's a rare find for ten dollars. If more wines like this were coming out of California, we would be much happier.

Nose Bright peach and delicate flowers mix with toast and yeast. One taster even imagined that it smelled like buttered lima beans.

Mouth Tasters found crisp apple, green pear, minerals, vanilla, caramel, and creamy wood—but nobody found it too oaky. The wine seemed to have a long somewhat floral finish. It's full bodied yet very well balanced.

Design It's not exciting; the light pink and mustard yellow colors would go well in a hospital room. Happily, though, it's not gaudy.

MORRO BAY
VINEYARDS
2006
CHARDONNAY
California

Mouton Cadet

Bordeaux, Barons Phillipe de Rothschild

Rank #12 of 39 light Old World reds under $15 tasted
Country France **Vintage tasted** 2005
Grapes Merlot, Cabernet Sauvignon, Cabernet Franc
Drink with sandwiches, creamy pastas
Website www.bpdr.com

This bottle isn't just ubiquitous in the US; you'll see Mouton Cadet in liquor stores and supermarkets all over the world—even in towns, cities, and countries where wine is virtually impossible to find. As it turns out, this is a good thing for wine-craving travelers. It's an easy-to-drink dinner-party wine that comes off lighter than you might expect from a Bordeaux blend.

Nose There's a lot going on here; one taster called the nose overactive. There's some exotic spice and some earth. You'll find interesting and new aromas with each sniff.

Mouth It begins very Old World, with that slight animal-like taste and some dark cherry. The short and abrupt finish is a weak point, and, surprisingly, could use more acidity.

Design The goat creature evokes a set of dishware from a home decorating store in middle America. We prefer the 1940s bottles from this historic producer—check them out on the website.

Nathanson Creek Merlot

Rank #7 of 52 light New World reds under $15 tasted
Country United States **Vintage tasted** Non-vintage
Grapes Merlot
Drink with cheese and crackers before dinner, strawberries after

Nathanson Creek is owned by Constellation Wines, the largest wine company in the world. (It may be a behemoth, but at least they don't spend too much on marketing—check out chapter 4.) But our tasters loved this cheapo Merlot, giving it positive notes again and again. It's a good entry-level wine for a new drinker, and commonly available in magnums at an even better value than the regular bottle.

Nose Very simple aromas of cherry, strawberry, and other red fruits are hard not to like.

Mouth The fruit keeps up, along with hints of black pepper and a nice, long finish—a bit shocking in a six-dollar wine. Blind tasters also found it to be well balanced.

Design Ay ay ay. Two leaping frogs on one bottle? One would seem to be enough, even for the most diehard frog-lover. We like the shape, though; it's more bottle than you usually get for six dollars.

Nobilo Sauvignon Blanc

Rank #8 of 50 light New World whites under $15 tasted
Country New Zealand **Vintage tasted** 2006
Grapes Sauvignon Blanc
Drink with ceviche, fish carpaccio, citrus salad
Website www.nobilo.co.nz

Nobilo was founded in the 1940s by a Croatian immigrant whose family had been making wine in Europe for hundreds of years. According to the story, he moved to New Zealand in hopes of continuing to make wines in the Old World style—the likes of which were nowhere to be found in Kiwi country. The only problem is that the flavors in this wine have almost nothing to do with that story. The only European thing about this Sauvignon Blanc is its high acidity; otherwise, the Nobilo's tropical, heavy-handed flavors are very New World. Still, it's tart and refreshing, like a typical New Zealand Sauvignon Blanc should be.

Nose Blind tasters smelled not just the classic grapefruit, but also tropical fruit, and some minerals and grass. It's not quite as over-the-top with the "cat pee" or grass flavors as some New Zealand Sauvignon Blancs, but it's still unmistakably in the style.

Mouth The acidity comes on strong and suddenly. Tasters found more fruit than expected, especially peach.

Design It's simple and unusually refined for the New World, with a pleasing color combination and regal fonts. This bottle is a pleasure to look at and serve.

Osborne Solaz Tempranillo Cabernet Sauvignon

$9 WINNER

Rank #1 of 18 heavy Old World reds under $15 tasted
Country Spain **Vintage tasted** 2004
Grapes Tempranillo, Cabernet Sauvignon
Drink with braised meats, heavy stews
Website www.osbornesolaz.com

This is a rich, full-bodied, long-lasting blockbuster of a red wine from a company founded in 1772 that's best known for its Port. The value is extraordinary; the price can dip as low as $6. Osborne's well-endowed bull, which is plastered across roadside displays all over Spain, has become a national icon. In the 1980s, however, a law banned the use of advertising on highways, threatening the bulls. But Spaniards protested, and the bulls were allowed to stay, having been deemed part of the national landscape. How's *that* for brand loyalty?

Nose It's a nice sweet-and-savory combination of black fruit, candied cherries, cinnamon, and nutmeg.

Mouth It explodes in the mouth with Christmas-like spices and tannins to accompany the fruit.

Design The trademark bull headlines an old-meets-new look that works pretty well. Try to get your hands on one of their great wooden cases— they transport you to another age.

Oyster Bay Sauvignon Blanc

(\$13)

Rank #2 of 50 light New World whites under \$15 tasted
Country New Zealand **Region** Marlborough
Grapes Sauvignon Blanc, Chardonnay
Vintage tasted 2006
Drink with fish and chips, grilled shrimp
Website www.oysterbaywines.com

This wine is like a caricature of a New Zealand Sauvignon Blanc, whose flavors are often described in wine jargon as "gooseberry and elderflower." We'll refrain from using those words, as we know few people who have actually eaten or smelled either of the above. Instead, our blind tasters described it as being crisp, pure, vigorous, and citrusy, with a hyper-strong New Zealandy aroma and taste. In other words, it's got all the qualities one looks for in a wine of this style, but they've been exaggerated.

Nose It's bright, with almost glaring versions of the grapefruit, lime, and grassy aromas you'd expect.

Mouth An ever-so-slight prickle accompanies the sharp acidity that screams New Zealand.

Design The label seems to be influenced by Hallmark sympathy cards. A black-and-white bay—more of a cove, really—sits quietly behind tacky calligraphy. The only thing missing is Für Elise.

Parducci Sustainable Red
Mendocino Wine Co.

$11

Rank #2 of 52 light New World reds under $15 tasted
Country United States **Vintage tasted** 2005
Grapes Merlot, Cabernet Sauvignon, Syrah, Zinfandel
Drink with chiles rellenos, duck breast with fruit sauce
Website www.mendocinowinecompany.com

This is a wine you can definitely feel good about buying. As the name implies, these people are committed to sustainable winemaking, but it seems they're not sacrificing quality in the process. Among the several grapes in this big blend, Cabernet Sauvignon comes out as the dominant flavor. Almost all of our tasters commented on the aromas and flavors of vegetables, which is common for young Cabernet. Happily, the Syrah and Zinfandel don't come on too sweet.

Nose The vegetal aromas are dominated by green pepper. One taster smelled stewed tomatoes.

Mouth It's a little sweet at first, but a second taste reveals more balance. Tasters found fresh berries, fruit, and licorice.

Design The tree-like vine is lovingly rendered—the idea, of course, is to imagine that the it's from one of the family-owned farms where the Sustainable Red's grapes are grown.

Parducci Sustainable White

Mendocino Wine Company

$11

WINNER

Rank #1 of 50 light New World whites under $15 tasted
Country United States **Vintage tasted** 2007
Grapes Sauvignon Blanc, Muscat Canelli, Tokai, Viognier
Drink with seared tuna, Asian fusion dishes
Website www.mendocinowinecompany.com

This brand-new arrival is bright, lively, and surpassingly complex, a great outdoor picnic bottle that gives you a lot of flavors to think about. What's even more exciting about this independently owned winery is its devotion to local farmers and its groundbreaking commitment to earth-friendly packaging, solar power, and carbon neutrality.

Nose The aromatic Muscat Canelli and Tokai grapes make it uniquely peachy and flowery—but, in spite of the aromatic Viognier in the mix, too, it doesn't go too far.

Mouth Blind tasters lauded the wine's refreshing mix of green apple and tangerine flavors, which add to the grapefruit, citrus, and nice acidity that you'd expect from Sauvignon Blanc; some even noticed a slight prickle. Believe it or not, two of our judges independently found notes of orange creamsicle.

Design It's tasteful and restrained. Recycled paper adds a fun texture to the well designed label.

Parallèle 45 Côtes du Rhône Blanc ($12)

Paul Jaboulet Aîné

Rank #3 of 15 heavy Old World whites under $15 tasted
Country France **Vintage tasted** 2006
Grapes Grenache blanc, Marsanne, Viognier, Bourboulenc
Drink with pastas with cream sauces, risotto
Website www.jaboulet.com

A powerhouse in France producing wines in most of the Rhône Valley appellations, Paul Jaboulet Aîné has ventured into the lower-priced everyday market with their Parallèle 45 line—so named because the vines run across the 45th parallel. They seem to have struck a chord with US consumers looking for cheap French wines—not easy to find these days—and with our blind tasters, who loved this wine's unusually harmonious balance. The Parallèle 45 white easily outperformed its red sibling.

Nose It's bright with fruit, especially peach. Blind tasters also identified tropical fruits.

Mouth The fruitiness—more peach, plus maybe some apple—is nicely set against steely acidity. This is the very definition of a well-balanced inexpensive white.

Design Jaboulet has replaced the classic French label with a well-conceived version that fuses the new with the old. The bottle deftly avoids busy graphics and stays elegant.

Parallèle 45 Côtes du Rhône Rosé

Paul Jaboulet Aîné

Rank #1 of 29 rosés under $15 tasted
Country France **Vintage tasted** 2006
Grapes Grenache, Cinsault, Syrah
Drink with a shellfish platter on the beach
Website www.jaboulet.com

In Europe, dry rosé wine is the nectar of the affluent beach holiday, the classic accompaniment to seaside seafood. You'll find the world's wealthiest men drinking it in Saint-Tropez. In America, on the other hand, rosé is associated with that cloying "blush" wine (e.g. White Zinfandel) that no male would be caught dead drinking. This Côtes du Rhône rosé from southern France is in the former category: it's pleasantly dry, refreshing, and ideal for drinking outdoors on a hot summer day. We wish there were more readily available rosés like this.

Nose The scent is fairly faint, dominated by light red fruit.

Mouth Many blind tasters found the acidity to be a bit high, and it is—enjoy the pleasant change from low-acidity American rosé.

Design The new design from Jaboulet works particularly well against the lovely salmon color of the wine. This is a bottle you can proudly pour at a pretentious garden party.

Perrin Côtes du Rhône Réserve

Perrin & Fils

Rank #5 of 18 heavy Old World reds under $15 tasted
Country France **Vintage tasted** 2005
Grapes Grenache, Syrah, Mourvèdre
Drink with a cheese plate, roast chicken, or nothing at all
Website www.perrin-et-fils.com

This is a party wine. As one of our blind tasters pointed out, the easy-to-enjoy aromas and tastes practically scream, "drink me." The Perrin does well with food, but it might fare even better by itself; it doesn't have the texture to stand up to heavy dishes. If you like New World wine, this fruity Rhône wine is an easy foray into the Old World.

Nose There's a lot here, even if it's nothing unique: intense black cherry, spice, and a fruit-forwardness we'd typically associate more with New World wine.

Mouth The taste is fresh, fruity, young, and not so Old World— except for its nice dose of acidity. There's some tannin, too. Some people tasted licorice on the surprisingly lengthy finish.

Design The Burgundy bottle shape is nice, but the goofily upward-angled script looks as though it comes from an overpriced restaurant menu.

Petit Bistro Cabernet Sauvignon

Rank #7 of 18 heavy Old World reds under $15 tasted
Country France **Vintage tasted** 2005
Grapes Cabernet Sauvignon
Drink with pork chops, thick vegetable soup

At first glance, Petit Bistro seems like some sort of New World wine going for a fake European aesthetic. Turns out it's a French wine going for a fake European aesthetic. And while the liquid itself doesn't do much to convince you of its Euro lineage, it's not bad. You'll get a laugh out of the preposterous text on the back of the bottle, which reminds us of those old TV ads for General Foods International Coffees; we won't spoil the surprise here.

Nose It's somewhat faint, but tasters did find hints of berries.

Mouth The wine manages to have lots of fruit without being too sweet. It's slightly tannic, but a couple of blind tasters found the effect somewhat fake or synthetic.

Design The daydream-inducing label is going for that Van Gogh Starry Night look, and we're kind of embarrassed to admit that we actually like it. The nice, warm vibes will make you daydream your way to France—or, at least, to Epcot.

Pirovano Montepulciano d'Abruzzo

Rank #10 of 39 light Old World reds under $15 tasted
Country Italy **Vintage tasted** 2004
Grapes Montepulciano
Drink with a plate of cured meats and cheeses
Website www.vinicantinepirovano.com

If you're a seasoned Italophile, don't be confused; in this case, Montepulciano refers to the grape, not the Tuscan hilltown—it's not to be confused with the more expensive Vino Nobile de Montepulciano. Happily, Pirovano's attractive and modern facilities have created a good wine from humble origins: the poor central-southern region of Abruzzo. It's a light-bodied wine with nice balance: we'd happily sit and sip this for a few hours with good company.

Nose There's some fruit, like currant and plum, as well as what one taster described as an old-attic smell—we find that typical of the old-school Italian winemaking technique and equipment.

Mouth A good balance of fruit and earth make up this soft wine. It's got an unusually good finish that reminded one taster of dried cherry and orange peel.

Design The frescoed label plays on an idyllic image of the Italian Renaissance, which isn't as convincing for us as the bottle's contents.

Porcupine Ridge Sauvignon Blanc

West Coast Origin

Rank #13 of 50 light New World whites under $15 tasted
Country South Africa Vintage tasted 2006
Grapes Sauvignon Blanc, Semillon
Drink with Indian curry, fried catfish, oyster po' boy

Unlike its label, this wine speaks softly. It's a straightforward, low-intensity wine whose flavor profile is subtle and pleasing; you'll find that it grows on you over time. Definitely let the bottle sit for a few minutes after opening and before drinking. This bottle suffers from a common problem with screw-cap wines, which are commonly bottled with a higher proportion of sulfites than other bottles; if you don't let it breathe, you might get aromas evocative of wet paint.

Nose There are the requisite Sauvignon Blanc aromas of grass and what's often described as cooked cabbage.

Mouth Refreshing flavors of green apple combine with crisp acidity.

Design You'll love it or hate it. The porcupine's apologists would point to the fact that it's less offensive than most critter-wine bottles. Its detractors, though, are turned off by the spikes, which don't exactly put you in a wine-drinking mood.

Presto Prosecco Brut

$10

Rank #6 of 22 sparkling wines under $15 tasted
Country Italy **Vintage tasted** Non-vintage
Grapes Prosecco
Drink with cured meats, smoked fish, or by itself

Crisp, appley, and festive, this Italian sparkler reminded our blind tasters strongly of hard cider—but good, dry hard cider, not that artificially sweet Cider Jack-type stuff. For some tasters, it even brought to mind a Belgian white ale. The Presto has only 11% alcohol, so it's ideal as an apéritif.

Nose Green apples and spices dominate the simple, pleasant aromas. The wine is better suited to relaxed celebrating than to pompous sniffing.

Mouth Because of the noticeably low acidity, the mouth-filling apple and pear flavors come off sweeter in the mouth than they do on the nose. The bubbles are a bit coarse but still fun.

Design What a pretty bottle. We love its voluptuous shape, sparse verbiage, and restrained look—no starbursts or coats-of-arms here. Plus, it's hard for us not to like the color of the label: Fearless Critic orange.

Red Truck Petite Sirah

Rank #18 of 135 heavy New World reds under $15 tasted
Country United States **Vintage tasted** 2006
Grapes Petite Sirah
Drink with spaghetti with meatballs, duck breast
Website www.redtruckwine.com

This wine's marketing pitch has a lot of Americana to it—which is why we were amused to learn that the winemaker is of Greek-Italian descent. Maybe that explains his pleasantly restrained winemaking technique. This isn't the only Red Truck wine we tasted; we also tried the Red Truck Red, a blend whose excessive sweetness pushed it out of the top 100. This Petite Sirah, however, is more restrained—and its grapes are organically grown. What's not to like about that?

Nose Tasters found an earthiness (dirt, roots, and fertilizer), some sweet spice (cinnamon and nutmeg), and fruit (raspberry and blueberry).

Mouth Lots of dark fruit is balanced a bit by a touch of tannin on the finish. Tasters found strawberry and even the taste of root beer.

Design It looks like *The Grapes of Wrath* has gone glamorous. No crop-ruining dust storms here—just sunny California days and concentrated Petite Sirah.

Redwood Creek Cabernet Sauvignon $8

Rank #16 of 135 heavy New World reds under $15 tasted
Country United States **Vintage tasted** 2005
Grapes Cabernet Sauvignon
Drink with broiled steak, osso buco, tagine
Website www.redwoodcreek.com

Visit the company website, and you'd think Redwood Creek was a retailer of sporting goods; there seems to be a bigger initiative underway to promote rock climbing, canoeing, and camping than drinking. But the winery might be selling itself short, as this wine is a nice surprise. It's a classic version of a bold, heavy California Cabernet. Not that there's anything wrong with that—when it's done right.

Nose Our blind tasters loved the nose, especially the hints of strawberry rhubarb pie; baked apples; and dark, stewed fruit.

Mouth It's dark, chocolaty, and coffee-esque. Use your imagination, and you might taste maple, too—but the finish is short.

Design A rushing river conjures up whitewater rafting, and the rugged texture of the paper seems to ensure that it could survive a day in a North Face trekking pack.

ADD

René Barbier Mediterranean Red

$6

Catalunya

Rank #8 of 39 light Old World reds under $15 tasted
Country Spain **Vintage tasted** Non-vintage
Grapes Tempranillo, Garnacha, Monastrell
Drink with grilled lamb chops, hamburgers
Website www.renebarbier.com

"Chair wine," as we like to call it, is one of those bottles that you'll often see staring up from the most bargain of the bargain bins. If you hit a store with the right overstock, three for ten dollars is not unheard of, which is why it makes us so happy that the wine's actually good. Its light, simple, spicy drinkability makes it more pleasant than a lot of California fruit bombs selling for five times the price. This is a red you could serve chilled— and a red you could drink three bottles of before you notice.

Nose Green and black pepper are all over the place.

Mouth There's pepper here, too, and acidity. Blind tasters liked its light body and pleasant simplicity.

Design The lone seaside chair and sunset have nostalgic meaning to Robin. This was the wine with which his high school friend, Meg, taught him to drink—and to live well.

Robert Mondavi Pinot Noir

Private Selection, Central Coast

Rank #6 of 52 light New World reds under $15 tasted
Country United States **Vintage tasted** 2005
Grapes Pinot Noir
Drink with Thanksgiving dinner, take-out pizza
Website www.rmprivateselection.com

Everybody knows Robert Mondavi. He's a presence on mid-level wine lists, in supermarket wine sections, and in homes all across America. Is this status deserved? Well, when we put this Pinot Noir in a brown paper bag, people loved it. No one thought it was expensive—some even identified it as a cheap Pinot—but that wasn't held against it. However, Mondavi's performance in our tastings at large was less impressive: this was the only one of 14 under-$15 Mondavi wines tasted to make the top 100.

Nose It's nice and inviting, full of soft fruit and gentle sweet spice.

Mouth More gentle fruit softly shows up, and the finish is nice, but the acidity could be higher. This wine doesn't have the balance of the classic colder-weather Pinot Noir.

Design We've got some advice for Mondavi: you're a household name, so don't cheapen your wine. Do away with the lighthouse shrouded in clouds and silly-looking calligraphy.

Rosemount Shiraz
Diamond Label

Rank #22 of 135 heavy New World reds under $15 tasted
Country Australia **Vintage tasted** 2005
Grapes Shiraz
Drink with meatloaf, braised lamb shank, short ribs
Website www.rosemountestate.com

Ever seen the Rosemount TV commercials? Borrowing heavily from luxury car ads, they feature sleek, sexy wine bottles from all angles, and proclaim Rosemount to be a "diamond worth discovering." Turns out that as far as cheap Shiraz goes, it actually is. This is a big wine with warm cooked fruit flavors and surprising balance, at least when compared with the abominable sweetness of most of its kin. To wit: the Rosemount is the only one of 17 bottles of Aussie Shiraz tasted to make the top 100.

Nose It's very fruit forward, with that Shiraz sour cherry, plus strong dried fruit and compote.

Mouth Blind tasters noticed even more stewed fruit here: prunes, blackberries, and such.

Design Rosemount's trademark square-bottomed bottle shape ensures that it won't go unnoticed on the shelves. Sexy or not, there's something sinister and threatening about all that black.

Rotari Brut
Metodo Classico, Trento DOC

$13

Rank #3 of 22 sparkling wines under $15 tasted
Country Italy **Vintage tasted** Non-vintage
Grapes Chardonnay, Pinot Noir
Drink with spicy Thai dishes, chocolate brownie

Don't call it Prosecco: this Brut from northern Italy is a nice departure from the Italian bubblies you're used to seeing in the $15-and-under sparkling category. The regions of Trentino and Lombardy are big but underappreciated producers of elegant sparkling wines, and this creamy, fun-to-drink Rotari is a poor man's Ferrari (not the car, but the legendary Trentino sparkling wine producer).

Nose It's creamier than most inexpensive sparklers; its aromas are more reminiscent of Crémant or Champagne, but there's some apple here, too.

Mouth The bubbles are a bit loose and unrefined. The flavor comes on a little sweeter than expected, but there's good acidity to balance it out, and a pleasant finish.

Design Simplicity wins in this bottle with the elegant yellow label—it's a far cry from Korbel. This is dignified Northern Italian design, aging gracefully.

Samos Muscat

Kourtaki

Rank #1 of 51 sweet and aromatic wines under $15 tasted
Country Greece **Vintage tasted** Non-vintage
Grapes Muscat
Drink with blue cheese and honey, roasted nuts
Website www.nestorimports.com

The deep golden color and lovely viscosity of this dessert wine are just part of what makes it a great way to end the night. What we love even more is the delicate sugar-acid balance. Just as you're being serenaded by sweet honey and apricot flavors, that mouth-watering acidity counterbalances the finish. Plus, the wine is made on the island of Samos in the Aegean Sea—that ought to impress your dinner guests.

Nose The honeyed and olive-brine aromas make for a more interesting combination than most simple Muscat wines; this reminded tasters of something far more expensive.

Mouth It's filling, with a long aftertaste and lovely flavors of honey and sour apple—and then there's that welcome acidity, too.

Design There's an interesting monochromatic effect from the similarities between the gold label and the color of the wine; for that, we'll forgive it the rest.

Santa Cristina

Antinori, Toscana IGT

Rank #6 of 39 light Old World reds under $15 tasted
Country Italy **Vintage tasted** 2005
Grapes Sangiovese, Merlot
Drink with red-sauce pasta, Wiener schnitzel
Website www.antinori.it

Antinori was one of the early popularizers of so-called "Super-Tuscans"—pricey blends of traditional Tuscan Sangiovese with international grapes to create highly concentrated, distinctly un-Italian wines designed to appeal to the Robert Parkers of the world. Happily, this poor man's Super-Tuscan doesn't fall victim to over-fruitiness; if anything, it errs on the opposite side. Certainly it's more complex than your old straw Chianti bottle, but in Italy, this is a simple table wine, so it's a bit steep at $10. Here's hoping for a speedy US dollar recovery.

Nose The delicate soft red fruits and slightly vegetal notes are somewhat pedestrian.

Mouth It's well balanced between acidity and tannin, and it also has flavors of dried cherry. Many found the finish a little too short.

Design Everything's pretty straightforward and restrained on this bottle. At least there's nothing outwardly ugly.

Santi Pinot Grigio

Sortesele

Rank #8 of 21 light Old World whites under $15 tasted
Country Italy Vintage tasted 2005
Grapes Pinot Grigio
Drink with fish in light sauce, risotto, cheddar cheese

We're often frustrated by mass-market Italian Pinot Grigio. It's rarely particularly bad, and it usually has decent acidity, but it often feels a bit inert. Santi more or less fits that description, but it's one of the better Pinot Grigio values. What we like is that it's easy to drink on its own. In fact, pairing it with food can be a bit challenging, as many dishes will overpower it. Keep in mind, though, that Italians don't actually drink much Pinot Grigio. It's made mostly for export.

Nose Among the inoffensive aromas, our blind tasters noticed vanilla, minerals, and green fruit.

Mouth Tropical fruit flavors complement the steely, metallic body and crisp acidity.

Design Froof. A goofy, gold-lacy bar running across the top and bottom of the label evokes a great-grandmother's old china, while the cursive and coat-of-arms are hilariously misdirected attempts at pomposity.

Segura Viudas Brut Reserva

$8

Rank #5 of 22 sparkling wines under $15 tasted
Country Spain **Vintage tasted** Non-vintage
Grapes Macabeo, Parellada, Xarel-lo
Drink with salmon mousse, octopus, fresh fruit

Great values are coming out of Spain, and Cavas are some of the best. They're sold for a fraction of the price of their similarly made French counterparts—and our blind tasters often thought they were just as good, if not better. This is one of the cheapest versions on the market; even if it's the low price that sells, the wine holds up admirably.

Nose There's definitely apple here, as there is in many Cavas, but some blind tasters also noticed pear, bread, and mineral flavors.

Mouth The mouth and nose seem to be in balance. That is, the wine tastes the way it smells: apple, pear, bread, minerals. There's good, crisp acidity, too.

Design Cheaply gilded trim, muddy purples and maroons, and too many fonts, logos, labels, and coats of arms totally fail to create the image of royalty that Segura Viudas seems to have had in mind. No kings or queens here; this is strictly petty nobility.

Sincerely Sauvignon Blanc

Neil Ellis

Rank #5 of 50 light New World whites under $15 tasted
Country South Africa Vintage tasted 2006
Grapes Sauvignon Blanc
Drink with smoked fish, grilled cheese sandwiches
Website www.neilellis.com

Bright and lively, this screwcap wine is indeed a sincere version of South African Sauvignon Blanc. Our tasters were divided about its intensity; some loved it, while others found it simply too much. It's got strong grassy flavors typical of Sauvignon Blanc, as well as a healthy dose of acidity—but none of the mouth-puckering grapefruitiness of a New Zealand version. Some blind tasters found the vivaciousness of the mouth to be a jarring contrast to the somewhat faint nose.

Nose It's slightly floral, but you have to sniff really hard—putting your nostrils in peril of getting soaked—to get much else.

Mouth This is where the Sincerely shines. The mouth is much spunkier than the nose, with bold tropical fruit and flowers, yet plenty of acidity to keep it balanced.

Design It looks like something you might run across in an antique shop, with that letter-closing script and fleur de lis. But its simplicity saves it.

Terrazas de los Andes Malbec

Bodegas Terrazas

$10

Rank #4 of 135 heavy New World reds under $15 tasted
Country Argentina **Vintage tasted** 2006
Grapes Malbec
Drink with mixed grill, cassoulet
Website www.terrazasdelosandes.com

Bodegas Terrazas, so named for the terraced land on which the vines are planted, faces unique challenges related to the differing altitudes of each terrace. In their years of experience, they've managed to figure out what grows best where; they seem to be doing something right with the Malbec grape, as this deep, dark wine managed to beat out all of its Argentine counterparts in our tastings. Don't let us wax too poetic, though; one blind taster was jerked back into reality by the finish, saying it was a reminder that this still is a cheap wine fit for a cheap date.

Nose It's pleasant enough, with a fruity cherry aroma and a bit of black pepper.

Mouth People loved the fruit more than the oak, which reminded one taster of plywood.

Design They sure are proud of the Andes; they're plastered on most Terrazas wine bottles, and this one is no exception.

3 Blind Moose Chardonnay

$11

Rank #3 of 89 heavy New World whites under $15 tasted
Country United States **Vintage tasted** 2005
Grapes Chardonnay
Drink with raw salmon, lobster, apples with cheddar cheese
Website www.3blindmoose.com

The name sounds like it's designed for 10-year-olds, and the website looks that way too; apparently, these critters are studying for their Mooster of Wine. You can even amoose yourself and buy a 3 Blind Moose polo shirt—charging it to your MoosterCard, of course. Shockingly, these children's-book-author wannabes apparently still have the time to make some decent wine, and this California Chardonnay is most definitely above average, even if it's done in that classic overbearing style. And we have to award points for the only wine to feature blind tasting on the label.

Nose One taster said it smelled like angel food cake and pears; another found hints of stewed lemons.

Mouth The flavor reminded one taster of the vinyl swimming pool of her childhood. For other, less imaginative tasters, it was full of fruit—some deemed it overripe.

Design Was a blind moose employed for graphic design, too?

35° South Sauvignon Blanc

$9

Viña San Pedro

Rank #10 of 50 light New World whites under $15 tasted
Country Chile **Vintage tasted** 2006
Grapes Sauvignon Blanc
Drink with fried oysters, panini, mixed green salad
Website www.sanpedro.cl

The Southern Hemisphere's 35th parallel isn't a bad place to grow grapes—especially Sauvignon Blanc. The finished product manages to take on that "cat pee" smell that so characterizes the grape. It's a repulsive image, but the description works; otherwise, we can't think of a better way to describe the aromas than, "uh, smells like Sauvignon Blanc." To paraphrase Jesse Helms, you know it when you smell it; it's one of the most distinct aromatic profiles in the wine world, and one that pairs well with fried foods or lighter fare.

Nose Multiple blind tasters thought the wine smelled like grass—which is unsurprising in a Sauvignon Blanc.

Mouth The tastes are much stronger and livelier than the smells; there's a lot of citrus here.

Design The label manages to pull off a navigational theme, borrowing from the look of old maps, without coming off too buffoon-like. Bright touches of orange liven things up.

Trackers Crossing Chardonnay 365　$7

Rank #4 of 89 heavy New World whites under $15 tasted
Country Australia **Vintage tasted** 2006
Grapes Chardonnay
Drink with mussels and french fries

You might recognize the 365 brand from Whole Foods; it covers a range of proprietary products, from frozen vegetables to bread mixes to vitamin supplements. The 365 foray into wine has been successful indeed; the Trackers Crossing is one of several wines in the line that our tasters liked. You would never guess that this delicate wine is actually a Chardonnay from Australia, as it demonstrates spectacular restraint and balance.

Nose Tasters found delicate fruit aromas of peach, nectarine, melon, cantaloupe, and apple as well as a slight minerality.

Mouth Pear, apple, lemon, and more minerals dominate. A couple of tasters found an initial rubbery or plasticky note, but it quickly subsided as the balancing acidity took over.

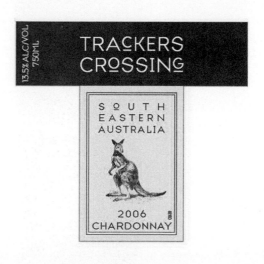

Design It wouldn't be an inexpensive Aussie wine without the kangaroo image. This one's kind of cute, though, and we like the font, which reminds us of a movie poster or Disney ride.

Trapiche Malbec

Rank #10 of 135 heavy New World reds under $15 tasted
Country Argentina **Vintage tasted** 2004
Grapes Malbec
Drink with grilled steak, blood sausage, sweetbreads

This is a big Argentine wine with bold tannins, making it a bit challenging to drink on its own. Pair it with food, though—ideally, a big grilled steak dinner—and you'll have some delicious results. The protein tames the tannin, and the end result is a happy marriage of juicy flavors and textures.

Nose It's powerful—very big and jammy with hints of cassis. You don't have to stick your nose way in to smell this wine.

Mouth It's quite tannic and has big, chocolaty flavors, but the finish is a bit of a letdown; some blind tasters seem to have been stuck with an unhappy aftertaste.

Design Argentines are an intensely stylish people, so we think they could do better than this. We don't mind the mountainous landscape and soaring bird, but it's placement beneath all the text seems incoherent. But we do love the heavy, tapered bottle.

Vida Orgánica Malbec

$9

Rank #15 of 135 heavy New World reds under $15 tasted
Country Argentina Vintage tasted 2006
Grapes Malbec
Drink with grilled steak, hamburgers, sautéed spinach

This Malbec, made from organically grown grapes in the Mendoza region of Argentina, is nice and simple for a New World wine, with an invigorating blend of fruit and spice. Like the winemaking philosophy, its flavors are unusually green, perhaps in part because it's so young.

Nose Rich and full aromas of black cherry and raspberry mix with herbal notes. Multiple blind tasters also smelled green pepper, and several were tricked into thinking this was a Cabernet.

Mouth A well balanced and soft palate full of blueberry fruit, some black pepper, and light tannins ends with a short finish.

Design The childish painting of a flower is touching; we're almost tempted to remove it and display it proudly on the refrigerator, as if our five-year-old had done it. The design scheme generally works, though especially against the substantial, ink-black bottle.

Villa Maria Sauvignon Blanc

Private Bin, Marlborough

(**$13**)

Rank #15 of 50 light New World whites under $15 tasted
Country New Zealand **Vintage tasted** 2007
Grapes Sauvignon Blanc
Drink with whole roasted fish, shrimp cocktail
Website www.villamaria.co.nz

Although the name sounds Italian or Spanish, Villa Maria is actually one of the big players in New Zealand. Most notably, this was the first winery in the world to do away with corks altogether, sealing their wines only with screwcaps. It's an interesting move, and we respect it—and so, increasingly, do consumers. As for the wine, it's a grassy Sauvignon Blanc, ideal for eating with seafood.

Nose A one-dimensional nose is all about grapefruit, lime, and that unmistakable Sauvignon-Blancness.

Mouth A briny, acidic quality led one taster to say that it tastes a bit like pickle juice. It's also got a slight prickle on the tongue, and big flavors with big acidity to match. The finish was universally loved.

Design The tasting note and pairing suggestions are right smack on the front of the bottle, taking away somewhat from its elegance. And we've got yet another coat-of-arms alert. Focus on the flavor.

Vin de Crete
Kourtaki

Rank #9 of 39 light Old World reds under $15 tasted
Country Greece **Vintage tasted** 2003
Grapes Kotsifali, Mandilaria
Drink with grilled lamb, fish with tomato-based sauce
Website www.nestorimports.com

For many, buying Greek wine, especially dry Greek wine, is a big mystery. It's a region relatively unknown even to wine aficionados, and there can be vast variations in quality. This one, however, is a great buy. This simple, harmonious, easy-to-drink European table wine feels and tastes rustic; it was clearly meant to be served with food.

Nose Nothing will jump out at you from the glass. There's a bit of bright red fruit, and what one blind taster identified as bubble gum.

Mouth It's light and acidic, with a short, slightly bitter finish that feels vaguely French.

Design It almost seems as if there's been effort put into making this label look outdated. Fake aged paper just ends up looking cheap, and a bullish creature in hieroglyphic style adds another cheesy, antiquated touch.

Vitiano

$9

Falesco, Umbria IGT

Rank #4 of 18 heavy Old World reds under $15 tasted
Country Italy **Vintage tasted** 2005
Grapes Cabernet Sauvignon, Merlot, Sangiovese
Drink with grilled lamb chops, steak, braised beef
Website www.falesco.it

As it mimics the Tuscan producers' newly acquired habit of blending international grapes like Cabernet Sauvignon and Merlot with the local grape varieties to create "Super-Tuscans," this wine might be dubbed a "Super-Umbrian." Umbria is Tuscany's neighbor, equally beautiful but less heralded by wine and travel magazines and cheesy book authors. Of the three grapes in the wine, our tasters picked up most on the Cabernet, with several noticing the smell and taste of green pepper.

Nose One blind taster described the aroma as mince pie, and others liked the aromas of vanilla.

Mouth There are definite tannins here; one taster said her mouth felt like it had been wiped dry with a towel.

Design It's not bad, it's just sad: the grapes are enumerated right on the front of the bottle, in accordance with New World labeling convention. As ever, we lament the death of tradition.

Five wine myths on trial
A wine importer corrects some common misperceptions

Myth 1: All rosé is sweet. The American wine industry ruined its own consumers' perception of rosé when we invented White Zinfandel. Now it's our responsibility to fix the problem by spreading the word that real rosé is dry rosé—the refreshing summer wine that's drunk by the elite of Europe, along the French Riviera, for the entire month of August.

Myth 2: All Merlot is bad. Consumption trends in the US wine market are spectacularly fickle; one year people are obsessed with one grape variety, and the next year, they're avoiding it like the plague. Lately, inspired by the film *Sideways*, the Merlot grape has been suffering through a fashion trough. There's still some bad California Merlot out there, but did you know that Château Pétrus, the most expensive wine in France, is almost entirely Merlot, too? It's not the grape, it's how you use it.

Myth 3: All Pinot Noir is good. Just because Pinot Noir is capable of subtle beauty when it's properly expressed doesn't mean you should buy it exclusively. In fact, the *Sideways* boom has brought some terrible wines to the market from places that Pinot should never be grown, like southern France and hot parts of California. Bad Pinot can be worse than no Pinot at all.

Myth 4: Restaurant markups are just a fact of life. It's fair for restaurants to take a reasonable profit when they sell wine, but they're *fleecing* you when they mark up wine by three or even four times retail, which is becoming the US norm. In Europe, restaurant markup is rarely more than two times, and it's usually more like 50%. Don't stand for American wine markups; patronize the small but growing subset of restaurants that are bucking the trend and charging reasonable prices.

Myth 5: The more expensive the wine is, the better. Some spectacularly expensive wines are worth the money, but a whole lot aren't. If you don't believe me now, you will once you've finished this book.

–Brian DiMarco

The Wolftrap
Boekenhoutskloof

Rank #7 of 135 heavy New World reds under $15 tasted
Country South Africa **Vintage tasted** 2005
Grapes Merlot, Grenache, Malbec, Syrah, Cinsault
Drink with braised short ribs, French onion soup
Website www.boekenhoutskloof.co.za

South African wines are a distinct set. In certain reds, the nose can be dominated by a smell similar to band-aids, known to wine nerds as "brettanomyces," or "brett." It can lead some to deem the wine flawed, but this isn't generally the case. Brett is definitely there in The Wolftrap, a big, concentrated South African blend. It's a bottle that will age well, and look good in your cellar (or kitchen) doing so.

Nose Beyond brett, some wine jargonists identified a"barnyard" smell (think horses and hay). But deep fruit lies beneath.

Mouth The wine explodes into every crevice of the mouth with dark chocolate, dark fruits, and tannins. Age it, and the texture will soften after a couple years.

Design The regal wood-cut wolf, presented with simplicity and grace, forms the centerpiece of a heavy, tapered bottle whose overall look is simply beautiful. It shows us what a critter wine can be at its best.

Zardetto Prosecco

$11

Rank #7 of 22 sparkling wines under $15 tasted
Country Italy **Vintage tasted** Non-vintage
Grapes Prosecco
Drink with bagels and lox, smoked herring, lobster roll
Website www.zardettoprosecco.com

Zardetto is one of only two Proseccos that made it into our top 100, and it's one of the most widely distributed wines of its kind in the world. The Prosecco grape makes sparkling wines whose flavor profile is quite different from that of Champagne; it doesn't have the so-called "creamy mousse" that the wine establishment looks for in French sparklers. Rather, it's light-bodied and fruity, neither yeasty nor toasty—a lot like hard cider, in fact.

Nose First and foremost, tasters detected apples, but their descriptions covered lots of other fruit and citrus ground, too: pear, peach, lemon, and lime.

Mouth It's dry and harshly sparkling, with aggressive fizz and a short finish. The flavor reminded one taster of gumballs.

Design The jarring juxtaposition of two utterly unrelated 1980s-ish fonts is amusing, but hardly harmonious. And do they really need to write "bubbly" all over the foil?

Appendices

Appendix 1 Experimental design

By Jake Katz and Jay Emerson

Preferences about wine are notoriously fickle. Many factors can influence the sensory experience, including advertising, price, setting, accompanying food, companions, and so on. We tried to design a study that would allow us to estimate the quality of wines while avoiding bias from these factors. While we acknowledge the substantial practical challenges of coordinating the efforts of wine-consuming adults, we are confident that the organizers' attention to detail paid off.

We devised a large-scale double-blind experiment, where neither the tasters nor the servers knew the identity of the wines. The design offered tasters one to four separate six-bottle flights of red, white, sparkling, or rosé wines over a period of one to four hours. Most tasters participated in at least two flights. Each taster sampled the six wines in their flight(s) and assigned an overall rating to each wine, as well as a ranking of their relative preference for the wines in each flight. We chose Yellow Tail Shiraz and Yellow Tail Chardonnay, the world's two top-selling individual wines, as red and white controls, and we included at least one control wine within each red and white flight.

In all, we held 17 tastings in New York, Connecticut, Massachusetts, and Texas; a total of 560 wines were tasted. The venues ranged from casual bars to top restaurants, with 10 to 75 attendees at each tasting. The 507 tasters were unpaid volunteers and included chefs, food professionals, wine distributors, wine professionals, and everyday wine drinkers invited by the editors. We provided easy-to-use forms to allow the tasters to rate each wine on a scale of one to four, and rank each of the six wines in order of preference.

We structured the tastings to reduce outside influence, preserve the independence of each taster's preferences, and avoid other potential sources of bias, including palate desensitization. The bottles were brown-bagged to hide their identities, numbered, and placed into flights of six wines. Tasters chose where to sit, and either flights or tables were rotated to ensure that tasters sampled a different flight in each round. Sparkling and rosé flights were used less frequently. Servers were unaware of the identities of the wines, and tasters could not see the bottle labels; thus, the country of production, brand, and price could not influence their ratings. All tasters used the same glasses (Fearless Critic-customized, ISO-approved 155-mL tasting glasses).

Tasters were asked not to discuss the wines during the tasting on the flights, and not to taste in any particular order. Thus, the interaction of tasters within a group was kept to a reasonable minimum, establishing a fair degree of independence in the results. However, we acknowledge that friends did often choose to sit together, faces were made, and occasional discussions ensued; it would be practically impossible to ensure complete independence. It is generally accepted that intoxication decreases particularity, so tasters were asked to use the spittoon to keep intoxication to a minimum. Most tasters cooperated, because we made it clear that at the conclusion of the event (after the data were collected) the wines would be freely available for the tasters to drink as much as they wanted.

We used a simple test of each taster's consistency to determine how much weight each would receive in the calculation of the overall ratings of the wines; we called this the "twin-wine test." A majority of tasters unknowingly participated in the twin-wine test: within many of the red flights, we included two identical bottles of the red control wine (Yellow Tail Shiraz). We measured taster consistency according to their relative rankings of the control wines. For example, if a taster ranked the two bottles of control wines in consecutive order, (second and third in a flight of six, for example), then that taster received the maximum possible weight in our analysis. Conversely, if the two tastings of the control wine produced opposite extreme rankings (first and sixth in the same flight), then that taster received much lower weight. When tasters participated in multiple twin-wine tests, the results were averaged to arrive at their weight. A minority of tasters never experienced a twin-wine test (usually due to arriving at a tasting late or leaving early). In this case, we based their weight on the range of their ratings of the control wines from different flights, appropriately normalized. When fewer than two control wine tastings were available for a taster, we assigned the taster a weight slightly below the average weight of the other tasters (this applied to less than one-eighth of the individual wine tastings).

We were concerned that the diversity of venues could skew the results of the study, because many wines were only sampled on a single tasting date. One venue was of particular concern: Aquavit, an expensive, renowned restaurant in New York City, where we expected that the tasters might assign higher ratings than they would have in a different setting. However, there was no statistically significant evidence of site-bias at Aquavit. And in our final analysis, there was no evidence of any more general, statistically significant differences among the venues.

We were also concerned about differences between tasters, who fall into two general groups: well-educated professionals (including many Ivy League graduates) and wine and food industry experts. All of the tasters attended willingly and enthusiastically, but clearly the pool of tasters does not represent a typical or random swath of the general population of wine consumers. Thus, the conclusions of the study must be qualified as representing only the opinions of this curious, convenient, enthusiastic, and cooperative pool of tasters. However, we do suspect that our volunteers have much in common with the potential readers of this book.

We designed the tasting forms to collect background information, to be easy to understand and complete, and to encourage individuals to reveal their preferences in a variety of ways. The tasting forms can be found in chapter 7 of this book.

We asked tasters to rank the six wines in each flight, we used a simple, four-point rating system: 1 (bad), 2 (okay), 3 (good), and 4 (great). The design was motivated by certain principles of wine tasting as established by the WSET (Wine Spirits and Education Trust, the world's premier wine education organization): for example, tasters rated aroma, aroma intensity, taste, and taste intensity separately in addition to the overall rating. At the same time, we attempted to combat survey fatigue and the general tendency for people to choose middle-of-the-road answers (there was no "middle" rating in the scale from 1 to 4). Many tasters voiced their appreciation for the simplicity of the form design.

We used standard analysis of variance (ANOVA) techniques to estimate the "quality" of each wine based on the taster ratings. We controlled for differences between tasters (some tasters rated wines generally high or low, while others used the full range of ratings), and we weighted the ratings based on our measure of taster consistency, described earlier. We found no statistically significant venue effect. In the end, we produced a score for each wine that reflects an estimate of its quality as assessed by this particular pool of tasters. The differences *between* the top 100 wines described in this book are not of statistical significance—attempting to refine the ratings with greater precision would require many more tastings than were feasible. However, the wines in the top 100 were certainly judged to be superior to the bottom 100 wines—a useful conclusion given the general similarity in price among the 560 wines.

Data entry and preparation are a critical, but tedious and thankless, part of any statistical analysis. Alexis Herschkowitsch manually entered all data from the tasting forms into a spreadsheet. Jacopo Anselmi carefully scrubbed the data to check for unexpected values, identify and confirm inconsistencies, and clean other features. For data on retail price, Alexis and Jacopo collected prices directly from the producers and by searching for wines online.

Appendix 2 Experimental conclusions

By Johan Almenberg and Anna Dreber Almenberg

Contrary to what we might expect, people do not appreciate expensive wines more (when they are unaware of the price). In a sample of more than 6,000 blind tastings, we find that the correlation between price and overall rating is small and *negative*, suggesting that individuals on average enjoy more expensive wines slightly *less*. For people with wine training (hereafter, "experts"), however, we find indications of a positive correlation.

In the regression analysis, the dependent variable is the overall rating, measured on a scale from 1 to 4, with 4 being the highest rating. The price variable is the natural logarithm of the dollar price. (If we didn't do this, we would be expecting a one-dollar increase to have the same effect at the $5 price level as at the $50 price level; this seems counterintuitive. We do get the same qualitative results using the dollar prices, but the statistical significance of the coefficients deteriorates.)

We use an ordered probit estimator as well as a linear estimator (OLS). In both cases we use robust standard errors. The ordered probit estimator is particularly well suited to an ordinal dependent variable, but we find that OLS also performs well, and yields estimates that are easier to interpret. In any case, the two models generate highly consistent results.

We employ three model specifications, and run all three using both the ordered probit and the OLS estimator. In Model 1, we regress the overall rating assigned to wine i, by individual j, on the price of the wine. In Model 2, we allow for the possibility that wine "experts," such as sommeliers or people with professional wine training, rate wines in a different manner. We include a dummy variable for being an expert, as well as an interaction term for price and the expert dummy. In a linear regression, this allows both the intercept and the slope coefficient to differ for experts and non-experts. In terms of the linear model, we can write these two models as

(1) $y_i = \beta_0 + \beta_1 \ln(PRICE_i) + \varepsilon_i$

and

(2) $y_i = \beta_0 + \beta_1 \ln(PRICE_i) + \beta_2 EXPERT_j + \beta_3 \ln(PRICE_i) * EXPERT_j + \varepsilon_i$

If individuals found that more expensive wine tasted better, the correlation between overall rating and price would be positive. In our sample, this is not the case: the coefficient on price is *negative* regardless of whether we use ordered probit or OLS. The linear estimator offers an interpretation of the magnitude of the effect: when we estimate model 1 using OLS, the coefficient is about -0.04, implying that a 100% increase in the (natural) log of the price is associated with a 0.04 reduction in the overall rating. The negative effect is moderate, but statistically significant (*p*-value: 0.038).

Unlike the non-experts, experts assign as high, or higher, ratings to more expensive wines. The interaction term for price and being an expert is highly statistically significant throughout. Controlling for experts produces a larger negative effect of price for non-experts, with improved statistical significance (ordered probit/OLS *p*-values: 0.013/0.012).

In addition, experts assign overall ratings that are on average half a rating point lower (OLS coefficient on the expert dummy: -0.448, *p*-value < 0.001). Regardless of whether we use ordered probit or OLS, estimation of Model 2 indicates that the correlation between price and overall rating is positive—or, at any rate, non-negative—for experts. The "net" coefficient for experts is the sum of the coefficient on ln(price) and the coefficient on ln(price)*expert. With OLS, this is approximately 0.1 and marginally statistically significant (*p*-value: 0.09). For ordered probit, the net coefficient is about 0.11 and marginally statistically significant (*p*-value: 0.099). The price coefficient for non-experts is negative.

When we estimate Model 2 using OLS, the model predicts that for a wine that costs ten times more than another wine, if we were to use a 100-point scale (such as that used by *Wine Spectator*), the linear model predicts that for a wine that costs 10 times more than another wine, non-experts will on average assign an overall rating that is about four points *lower*, whereas experts will assign an overall rating that is about seven points *higher*. If the dollar price increases by a factor of 10, ln(price) increases by about 2.3. Hence the predicted effect on the overall rating of tenfold increase in the dollar price is 2.3 times the ln(price) coefficient for non-experts and experts, respectively.

We also test a third model, including individual fixed effects. Model 3 is essentially the same as Model 2, except that we add a dummy variable *j* for each individual taster. Including the fixed effects does not affect the qualitative results, and the coefficients themselves change only slightly. A Wald test rejects that the fixed effects are jointly equal to zero, by a wide margin (*p*-value < 0.001). All of these results apply regardless of whether we use ordered probit or OLS.

To make sure that our results are not driven by wines at the extreme ends of the price range, we also run our regressions on a reduced sample, omitting observations in the top and bottom deciles of the price distribution. Given the broad range of prices in the sample, this is an appropriate precaution. The wines in the reduced sample range in price from $6 to $15.

Using the reduced sample, we estimate Model 2 using both ordered probit and OLS, in each case with and without fixed effects. The qualitative results are highly consistent with those we get when using the full sample. In fact, the effects are larger, and the statistical significance improves further (*p*-value, non-expert price coefficient: 0.001).

Index

Acidity, 57

Alamos Malbec, 68

Alice White Chardonnay, 69

Almaden Chardonnay, 70

Almenberg, Johan, v, 9, 179

Amerine, Maynard, 9, 12, 34

Antinori, Santa Cristina, 157

Ariely, Dan, 13

Asimov, Eric, 28–29

Australian wines, 58

Authors and contributing
  writers, v

Avalon Cabernet Sauvignon, 71

Aveleda Vinho Verde, 72

Barbier, René, Mediterranean
  Red, 152

Barefoot Cabernet Sauvignon,
  73

Barefoot Merlot, 74

Bartoshuk, Linda, 31–32

Beaujolais-Villages, Georges
  Duboeuf, 110

Beringer Cabernet Sauvignon,
  75

Black Box Cabernet Sauvignon,
  76

Blind taste, 7

Blind tasters, ix

Blind tasting
  ours, 7, 39–47, 175-181
  yours, 49–52
  matchups, 53

Bogle Old Vine Zinfandel, 77

Bogle Sauvignon Blanc, 78

Bordeaux
  Château La Grange Clinet, 88
  Mouton Cadet, 136

Brochet, Fréderic, 11–12

Brut Reserva, Segura Viudas,
  159

Brut
  Domaine Ste. Michelle, 101
  Freixenet Cordon Negro, 106
  Lorikeet, 125
  Rotari, 155

Cabernet Sauvignon
  Avalon, 71
  Barefoot, 73

Beringer, 75
Black Box, 76
Charles Shaw, 86
Columbia Crest, 94
Cono Sur, 96
Liberty School, 123
Morro Bay, 133
Petit Bistro, 146
Redwood Creek, 151
Cáceres, Marqués de, Rioja
 Crianza, Red, 130
Cáceres, Marqués de, White
 Rioja, 129
Cadillac, 28
Campo Viejo Rioja Crianza, 79
Capitalism, 30
Carlo Rossi Paisano, 80
Casa Rey Malbec, 81
Casal Garcia Vinho Verde, 82
Castillo de Molina Pinot Noir,
 83
Cave de Lugny Mâcon-Villages,
 84
Cavit Merlot, 85
Chardonnay
 3 Blind Moose, 163
 Alice White, 69
 Almaden, 70
 Charles Shaw, 87
 Fat Bastard, 103
 Trackers Crossing, 365, 164
Charles Shaw Cabernet
 Sauvignon, 86
Charles Shaw Chardonnay, 87
Château La Grange Clinet, 88
Château Ste. Michelle Pinot
 Gris, 90
Château Ste. Michelle Riesling,
 91

Château Ste. Michelle
 Sauvignon Blanc, 92
Chianti, Malenchini, 127
Citra Pinot Grigio, 93
Columbia Crest Cabernet
 Sauvignon, 94
Concannon Petite Sirah, 95
Cono Sur Cabernet Sauvignon,
 96
Cono Sur Pinot Noir, 97
Constellation, 22, 137
Control states, 55
Cordon Negro, Freixenet, Brut,
 106
Cordon Negro, Freixenet, Extra
 Dry, 107
Côtes du Rhône
 Guigal, 113
 Perrin Réserve, 145
 Parallèle 45, Blanc, Jaboulet,
 141
 Parallèle 45, Rosé, Jaboulet,
 142
Cousiño Macul Riesling, 98
Crane Lake Sauvignon Blanc,
 99
Culture war, the, 31
Davis, Nat, v, 116
DiMarco, Brian, v, 170
Dom Pérignon, 3, 4, 7, 11, 21,
 29, 36, 100, 101
 new clothes, 19
Domaine Ste. Michelle Brut, 7–
 8, 21, 53, 66, 101
Dreber Almenberg, Anna, v, 9,
 179
Duboeuf, Georges, Beaujolais-
 Villages, 110
Dunster House, 1–2
Economist, The, 25

Editor's Picks, 57
  Aveleda Vinho Verde, 72
  Campo Viejo Rioja Crianza,
    79
  Freixenet Cordon Negro Brut,
    106
  House Wine, 115
Editors and contributors, vii
Emerson, Jay, v, 9, 39, 175
Experimental conclusions, 179–
  181
Experimental design, 175–178
Extra Dry, Freixenet Cordon
  Negro, 107
Falanghina, Feudi di San
  Gregorio, 105
Falesco Umbria, Vitiano, 169
Fâmega Vinho Verde, 102
Fat Bastard Chardonnay, 103
Faulkner, Julian, v, 39, 89
Fearless Critic Media titles, 134
Fetzer Valley Oaks Merlot, 104
Feudi di San Gregorio
  Falanghina, 105
Five wine myths on trial, 170
Frederick, Shane, 13
Freixenet Cordon Negro Brut,
  106
Freixenet Cordon Negro Extra
  Dry, 107
Full Circle Zinfandel, 108
Gato Negro Sauvignon Blanc,
  109
Georges Duboeuf Beaujolais-
  Villages, 110
Geyser Peak Sauvignon Blanc,
  111
Grand Pacific Starliner White,
  112
Grape Varieties, 57

Grüner Veltliner
  Huber Hugo, 117
  Lois, 124
Guigal Côtes du Rhône, 113
Harlow Ridge Pinot Grigio, 114
Heavy vs. light, distinction, 52–
  53, 57
House Wine, 115
Huber Hugo Grüner Veltliner,
  117
Hugo, Huber, Grüner Veltliner,
  117
Jaboulet, Parallèle 45 Côtes du
  Rhône Blanc, 141
Jaboulet, Parallèle 45 Côtes du
  Rhône Rosé, 142
Jay-Z, 28
Jindalee Estate Rosé, 118
Katz, Jake, v, 9, 39, 175
Kettmeir Pinot Grigio, 119
Kiwi Cuvée, 120
Kourtaki Mavrodaphne of
  Patras, 132
Kourtaki Samos Muscat, 156
Kourtaki Vin de Crete, 168
La Vieille Ferme Rouge, 121
LAN Rioja Crianza, 122
Latour, Louis, Le Pinot Noir, 126
Laube, James, 17
Lecocq, Sébastien, 10, 16
Lee, Leonard, 13
Liberty School Cabernet
  Sauvignon, 123
Light vs. heavy, distinction, 52–
  53, 57
Lois Grüner Veltliner, 124
Lorikeet Brut, 125
Louis Latour Le Pinot Noir, 126
Louis Vuitton Moët Hennessy, 4,
  21–23, 27, 100

Mâcon–Villages, Cave de Lugny, 84

Malbec
  Alamos, 68
  Casa Rey, 81
  Terrazas de los Andes, 161
  Trapiche, 165
  Vida Orgánica, 166

Malenchini Chianti, 127

Mark West Pinot Noir, 128

Marqués de Cáceres Rioja Crianza, Red, 130

Marqués de Cáceres White Rioja, 129

Marqués de Riscal Rioja, Rosé, 131

Mask and Spear Pub, The, 1–2, 5, 46

Mavrodaphne of Patras, 132

McCoy, Elin, 36

Mediterranean Red, René Barbier, 152

Mendocino Wine Co., Parducci Sustainable Red, 143

Mendocino Wine Co., Parducci Sustainable White, 144

Merlot, Barefoot, 74

Merlot
  Cavit, 85
  Fetzer Valley Oaks, 104
  Nathanson Creek, 137

Moët & Chandon, 11, 21-23, 100

Molina, Castillo de, Pinot Noir, 83

Mondavi, Robert, Pinot Noir, 153

Mondovino, film, 18

Montepulciano d'Abruzzo, Pirovano, 147

Morro Bay Cabernet Sauvignon, 133

Morro Bay Chardonnay, 135

Mouton Cadet, 136

Muscat, Samos, Kourtaki, 156

Nathanson Creek Merlot, 137

New World vs. Old World, distinction, 34–35, 52–53, 57

Nikki Beach, 20, 24

Nobilo Sauvignon Blanc, 138

Notes, 59

Old Vine Zinfandel, Bogle, 77

Old World vs. New World, distinction, 34–35, 52–53, 57

Osborne Solaz, 139

Oyster Bay Sauvignon Blanc, 140

Paisano, Carlo Rossi, 80

Parallèle 45 Côtes du Rhône Blanc, Jaboulet, 141

Parallèle 45 Côtes du Rhône Rosé, Jaboulet, 142

Parducci Sustainable Red, 143

Parducci Sustainable White, 144

Parker, Robert, 16–17, 34, 36

Perceptual learning, 32–34

Perfect palate, 15

Perrin Côtes du Rhône Réserve, 145

Petit Bistro Cabernet Sauvignon, 146

Petite Sirah
  Concannon, 95
  Red Truck, 150

Pinot Grigio
  Citra, 93
  Harlow Ridge, 114
  Kettmeir, 119
  Santi, 158

Pinot Gris, Château Ste. Michelle, 90
Pinot Noir
  Castillo de Molina, 83
  Cono Sur, 97
  Louis Latour, 126
  Mark West, 128
  Robert Mondavi, 153
Pirovano Montepulciano d'Abruzzo, 147
Placebo effect, 4, 13–14, 17–18, 19–21, 25, 30, 100, 128
Plassmann, Hilke, 10, 13–14, 25
Porcupine Ridge Sauvignon Blanc, 148
Preface: The wine haze, 1
Presto Prosecco Brut, 149
Prosecco
  Presto Brut, 149
  Zardetto, 172
Rangel, Antonio, 10, 13–14, 25
Red Truck Petite Sirah, 150
Redwood Creek Cabernet Sauvignon, 151
René Barbier Mediterranean Red, 152
Riesling
  Château Ste. Michelle, 91
  Cousiño Macul, 98
Rioja
  Campo Viejo Crianza, 79
  LAN, Crianza, 122
  Marqués de Cáceres, Crianza, Red, 130
  Marqués de Cáceres, White, 129
  Marqués de Riscal, Rosé, 131
Riscal, Marqués de, Rioja, Rosé, 131

Robert Mondavi Pinot Noir, 153
Robinson, Jancis, 9
Roessler, Edward, 9, 12, 34
Rosé, dry, 58, 170
Rosemount Shiraz, 154
Rossi, Carlo, Paisano, 80
Rotari Brut, 155
Rutherford, Grand Pacific Starliner White, 112
Samos Muscat, Kourtaki, 156
San Gregorio, Feudi di, Falanghina, 105
Santa Cristina, 157
Santi Pinot Grigio, 158
Sauvignon Blanc
  Bogle, 78
  Château Ste. Michelle, 92
  Crane Lake, 99
  Gato Negro, 109
  Geyser Peak, 111
  Nobilo, 138
  Oyster Bay, 140
  Porcupine Ridge, 148
  Sincerely, 160
  35° South, 162
Sauvignon Blanc, Villa Maria, 167
Scientific advisory board, vi
Segura Viudas Brut Reserva, 159
Seinfeld, Morty, 28
Shiraz, Rosemount, 154
Sincerely Sauvignon Blanc, 160
Smith, Adam, 30
So what, 25
Solaz, Osborne, 139
Starliner White, Grand Pacific, 112
Ste. Michelle, Château, Pinot Gris, 90

Ste. Michelle, Château, Riesling, 91

Ste. Michelle, Château, Sauvignon Blanc, 92

Ste. Michelle, Domaine, Brut, 101

Suckling, James, 18

Super-tasters, 31–32

Sustainable Red, Parducci, 143

Sustainable White, Parducci, 144

Tannins, 57

Taste of money, 11

Tasting form, 40, 49, 175–178

Tempranillo, Osborne Solaz, 139

Terrazas de los Andes Malbec, 161

The Wolftrap, 171

35° South Sauvignon Blanc, 162

3 Blind Moose Chardonnay, 163

365 Trackers Crossing Chardonnay, 164

Trackers Crossing Chardonnay 365, 164

Trader Joe's Charles Shaw Cabernet Sauvignon, 86

Trader Joe's Charles Shaw Chardonnay, 87

Trapiche Malbec, 165

Trials of a Young Winemaker, 89

Trials of pouring, 116

Two-Buck Chuck, Cabernet Sauvignon, 86

Two-Buck Chuck, Chardonnay, 87

Valley Oaks Merlot, Fetzer, 104

Verdict, The, 55

Veuve Clicquot, 21, 53

Vida Orgánica Malbec, 166

Vieille Ferme, La, Rouge, 121

Villa Maria Sauvignon Blanc, 167

Vin de Crete, 168

Vinho Verde
Aveleda, 72
Casal Garcia, 82
Fâmega, 102

Visser, Michael, 10, 16

Vitiano, Falesco Umbria, 169

Weinberg, Justin, 23

West, Mark, Pinot Noir, 128

White, Alice, Chardonnay, 69

Wine Enthusiast, 15

Wine reviews, 63

Wine Spectator, 10, 15–18, 29, 34, 36

Wine trials
ours, 7, 39–47, 175-181
yours, 49–52
matchups, 53

Winning wines, 63
Alice White Chardonnay, 69
Avalon Cabernet Sauvignon, 71
Domaine Ste. Michelle Brut, 101
Feudi di San Gregorio Falanghina, 105
LAN Rioja Crianza, 122
Mark West Pinot Noir, 128
Marqués de Cáceres White Rioja, 129
Osborne Solaz, 139
Parallèle 45 Côtes du Rhône Rosé, 142

Parducci Sustainable White,
144
Samos Muscat, 156
Wolftrap, The, 171
Yellow Tail, 3, 33, 35–36, 41,
175–176
Zardetto Prosecco, 172
Zinfandel
Bogle Old Vine, 77
Full Circle, 108

Notes